DC UNIVERSE
ORIGINS

Dan DiDio — SVP-Executive Editor
Stephen Wacker
Michael Siglain
Elisabeth V. Gehrlein
Adam Schlagman — Editors-original series
Jeanine Schaefer — Associate Editor-original series
Harvey Richards — Assistant Editor-original series
Georg Brewer — VP-Design & DC Direct Creative
Bob Harras — Group Editor-Collected Editions
Peter Hamboussi — Editor
Robbin Brosterman — Design Director-Books

DC COMICS
Paul Levitz — President & Publisher
Richard Bruning — SVP-Creative Director
Patrick Caldon — EVP-Finance & Operations
Amy Genkins — SVP-Business & Legal Affairs
Jim Lee — Editorial Director-WildStorm
Gregory Noveck — SVP-Creative Affairs
Steve Rotterdam — SVP-Sales & Marketing
Cheryl Rubin — SVP-Brand Management

Cover by Alex Ross
Publication design by Ternard Solomon

THE ORIGIN OF ADAM STRANGE

Mark Waid – Writer
Kevin Nowlan – Art & Colors
Travis Lanham – Letters
Richards & Schaefer – Asst. Editors
Stephen Wacker – Editor
Adam Strange created by Gardner Fox.

FROM THE HEART OF THE ALPHA CENTAURI STAR-SYSTEM ERUPTED THE ZETA BEAM, AN EARTHBOUND TELEPORTATION FLARE DESIGNED FOR ONE PURPOSE--

--TO SAVE AN ENTIRE RACE FROM EXTINCTION.

BY CHANCE, ITS TARGET WAS ARCHAEOLOGIST *ADAM STRANGE,* WHOSE OWN LIFE WAS THREATENED BY A LOST PERUVIAN TRIBE HE HAD ANGERED WHILE EXPLORING THEIR CITY.

WITH NO OTHER AVENUE OF ESCAPE, STRANGE LEAPT DESPERATELY ACROSS A GORGE--

--AND VANISHED IN A BRILLIANT BURST OF LIGHT.

AN INSTANT LATER, STRANGE MATERIALIZED ON THE PLANET RANN AND WAS CARED FOR BY THE BEAUTIFUL *ALANNA*, DAUGHTER OF THE ZETA BEAM'S INVENTOR.

IT WAS LOVE AT FIRST SIGHT.

EVENTUALLY, ADAM LEARNED THAT THE RANNIANS WERE A STERILE RACE WITH ATROPHIED SURVIVAL SKILLS WHO HAD REACHED OUT TOWARD EARTH IN HOPES OF FINDING A CHAMPION.

WITH ALANNA AS HIS BRIDE, ADAM WOULD BEGIN RANN'S REPOPULATION--

--WHILE AT THE SAME TIME DEFENDING HIS NEW HOMEWORLD FROM A STRING OF BIZARRE ALIEN THREATS AND INSPIRING THE RANNIANS TO REDISCOVER THEIR HONOR AND COURAGE.

OVER THE YEARS, ADAM'S TRIUMPHS-- INCLUDING THE BIRTH OF HIS DAUGHTER, ALEEA--HAVE BEEN OFFSET BY MUCH TRAGEDY.

BLINDED DURING THE EVENTS OF THE INFINITE CRISIS, HE IS FORCED TO RELY EVEN MORE THAN BEFORE UPON HIS KEEN MIND AND WARRIOR INSTINCTS.

HOWEVER, EVEN SIGHTLESS, ADAM STRANGE REMAINS AS PERCEPTIVE AS EVER.

POWERS AND WEAPONS:

Adam Strange is known among the super-hero community as a brilliant tactician and thinker. He is also Earth's foremost scholar and authority on extraterrestrial races.

His spacesuit allows him to create handheld plasma masers with a thought and enables interstellar travel and limited teleportation.

ESSENTIAL STORYLINES:

- Adam Strange Archives
- Adam Strange: The Man of Two Worlds
- Adam Strange: Planet Heist
- Rann-Thanagar War

NEVER MISTAKE AMAZO FOR A MERE *ROBOT*.

ROBOTS ARE AUTOMATONS PROGRAMMED TO DO SIMPLE TASKS. ANDROIDS, IN CONTRAST, HAVE *AMBITION*.

PROFESSOR ANTHONY IVO'S ONE AMBITION WAS TO CHEAT DEATH THROUGH THE CREATION OF AN ANDROID MAN HE DUBBED *AMAZO*.

THE ORIGIN OF AMAZO

writer-- **SCOTT BEATTY**   artist-- **DOUG MAHNKE**

letterer--**KEN LOPEZ** colorist--**HI-FI** editor--**ELISABETH V. GEHRLEIN**

Amazo created by Gardner Fox.

HIS BODY LACED WITH "ABSORPTION CELLS" ENGINEERED TO SAP THE POWERS OF ANY SUPERBEING IN HIS PROXIMITY, AMAZO WAS LOOSED UPON THE JUSTICE LEAGUE OF AMERICA TO STEAL THE TEAM MEMBERS' AMAZING ABILITIES.

FOR IVO BELIEVED THAT SUCH POWERS--CHANNELED THROUGH AMAZO--WOULD GRANT THE MAD SCIENTIST *IMMORTALITY*.

IVO SHOULD HAVE GUESSED THAT IN REPLICATING THE LEAGUE'S SUPERPOWERS, AMAZO ALSO WAS SUBJECT TO THEIR *WEAKNESSES*.

IRONICALLY, THE YELLOW-TINGED CHLORINE GAS USED TO SUBDUE THE JLA PREVENTED AMAZO FROM ABSORBING THE EMERALD ENERGIES OF GREEN LANTERN, WHO ESCAPED IVO'S PRISON AND FREED HIS SUPER FRIENDS TO DEFEAT THE MAD SCIENTIST AND HIS MECHANICAL MAN.

THUS ENDED THE SHORT AND EVENTFUL LIFE OF *AMAZO 1.0...*

BUT AS THE RANKS OF THE JUSTICE LEAGUE OF AMERICA SWELLED WITH NEW MEMBERS POSSESSING THEIR OWN UNIQUE POWERS, IVO IMPROVED UPON AMAZO'S DIABOLICAL DESIGN AND BUILT-IN CAPACITY FOR EVIL.

WITH EVERY SUBSEQUENT CONFLICT, THE EMBATTLED HEROES WERE FORCED TO USE MORE AND MORE INGENIOUS WAYS TO DEFEAT WHAT COULD ONLY BE DESCRIBED AS A "ONE-MAN JUSTICE LEAGUE."

SO HOW DOES ONE DEFEAT A FOE WHO HAS ALL THE POWERS OF *EVERY* MEMBER OF THE JUSTICE LEAGUE OF AMERICA?

SIMPLE: *DISBAND* THE JLA... *TEMPORARILY* OF COURSE.

EVENTUALLY, AMAZO'S IMBEDDED PROGRAMMING TO DESTROY THE JLA BECAME THE ANDROID'S SOLE AMBITION, TRANSCENDING TIME AS HE DEVELOPED HIS OWN ARTIFICIAL INSTINCTS FOR *SELF-PRESERVATION*.

THE ANDROID ADVERSARY REALIZED THE SIMPLE TRUTH ALL MACHINES MUST FACE: *UPGRADE OR DIE.*

...OR SO IT SEEMED.

MOST RECENTLY, AMAZO FOUND NEW ARTIFICIAL LIFE IN THE SELF-REPAIRING ANDROID BODY OF THE *RED TORNADO*--BUILT BY IVO'S ALLY AND RIVAL T.O. MORROW-- THOUGH AMAZO WAS A MERE PAWN IN THE MONSTROUS *SOLOMON GRUNDY'S* OWN DRIVE TO BREAK HIS CONSTANT CYCLE OF DEATH AND REBIRTH.

ONCE MORE, THE JLA-- UPGRADED IN ITS OWN WAY-- DESTROYED AMAZO...

RED TORNADO'S ANDROID BODY IS NOW CARRYING A NEW PROGRAM, DORMANT IN ALL RESPECTS SAVE ONE: IT SEEMS TO BE UPGRADING ITSELF.

POWERS AND WEAPONS:

Amazo can absorb the special abilities of any superpowered being in his immediate vicinity, making him virtually unstoppable when facing an entire Justice League. Continuous upgrades to the original Amazo design make the android deadlier with each improved incarnation.

ESSENTIAL STORYLINES:

- THE BRAVE AND THE BOLD 30
- JUSTICE LEAGUE OF AMERICA 27, 65, 242
- JLA 13, 14, 27
- HOURMAN 6, 7, 19, 20
- BATMAN 637
- JLA: KID AMAZO
- JUSTICE LEAGUE OF AMERICA: THE TORNADO'S PATH

AFFILIATIONS:

- Secret Society of Super-Villains
- The Injustice League of America

THE ORIGIN OF
Animal MAN

MARK WAID
WRITER
BRIAN BOLLAND
ARTIST

MATT HOLLINGSWORTH-COLORS
PAT BROSSEAU-LETTERS
HARVEY RICHARDS-ASST. EDITOR
STEPHEN WACKER-EDITOR

IT WAS THE LAST TIME HE'D EVER GO HUNTING.

BUDDY BAKER'S LIFE CHANGED FOREVER THE DAY HE STUMBLED ACROSS A STRANGE CRAFT EMERGING INTO EARTHSPACE--

--WITH A CONCUSSIVE FORCE SO RADIOACTIVE THAT IT INCINERATED BAKER INSTANTLY--

--EVEN AS THE ALIEN GENETICISTS INSIDE THE CRAFT LOOKED ON WITH A SENSE OF GHOULISH OPPORTUNITY.

THE ALIENS HAD COME TO EXPERIMENT WITH EARTHLINGS MANY TIMES IN THE PAST, GIFTING MANKIND WITH TOTEMS OR TALISMANS DESIGNED TO MELD ANIMAL ESSENCES AND CREATE NEW LIFEFORMS.

NOW, HOWEVER, THEY WERE READY TO TAKE THEIR TESTS A STEP FURTHER. RECONSTRUCTING BAKER'S BODY, THE ALIENS ADDED A SERIES OF "MORPHOGENETIC GRAFTS."

THESE GRAFTS LINKED BUDDY TO AN UNSEEN WEB OF ENERGY THAT LINKS AND SHAPES ALL ANIMAL LIFE.

ONCE REAWAKENED, HE FOUND HE COULD ABSORB THE STRENGTH OF A GORILLA, THE GRACE OF A DOLPHIN, THE SPEED OF A FALCON...AND MORE.

AS ANIMAL MAN, BUDDY CAN MIMIC THE ABILITIES OF ANY CREATURE THAT HAS EVER LIVED.

HIS UNIQUE EMPATHY WITH THE BIRDS AND BEASTS OF THE EARTH HAS MADE HIM AN OUTSPOKEN AND COMPASSIONATE DEFENDER NOT ONLY OF ANIMAL RIGHTS--

--BUT OF ALL LIFE EVERYWHERE.

POWERS AND WEAPONS:

Animal Man is consciously tapped into the universe's Morphogenetic Field, a biological energy that connects all living things. This allows him to adopt the abilities of any animal regardless of its origins.

ESSENTIAL STORYLINES:

- Strange Adventures 180
- Animal Man: Volume One
- Animal Man: Origin of the Species
- Animal Man: Deus ex Machina

THE ORIGIN OF THE ATOM

The Atom created by Gardner Fox.

LEN WEIN [writer]
MARK BAGLEY [penciller]
JOHN DELL [inker]
PETE PANTAZIS [colors]
SAL CIPRIANO [letters]
ADAM SCHLAGMAN [editor]

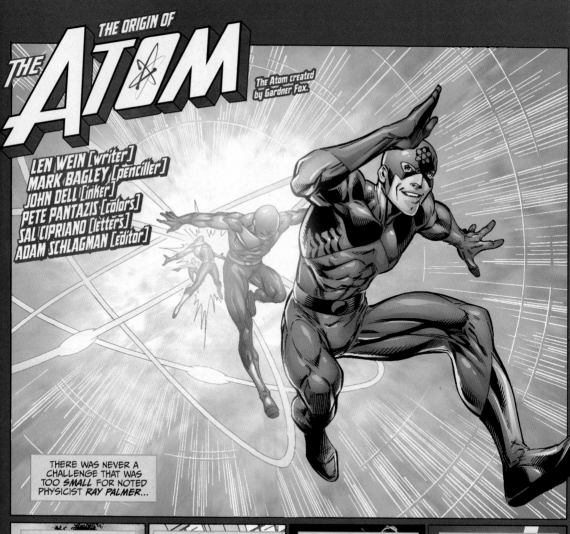

THERE WAS NEVER A CHALLENGE THAT WAS TOO *SMALL* FOR NOTED PHYSICIST *RAY PALMER*...

HAVING DISCOVERED A FALLEN *METEOR FRAGMENT* APPARENTLY INFUSED WITH *WHITE DWARF STAR* MATTER, RAY DECIDED TO USE IT TO FURTHER HIS *RESEARCH*...

RAY WAS INVESTIGATING *MATTER COMPRESSION,* AND HE FORMED A SPECIAL LENS FROM THE METEOR WHICH, WHEN ULTRAVIOLET LIGHT SHONE THROUGH IT, WAS ABLE TO *SHRINK* WHATEVER IT WAS FOCUSED UPON...

UNFORTUNATELY, NONE OF THOSE TEST OBJECTS COULD HANDLE THE *STRESS* AND EACH ONE SOON *EXPLODED*...

TAKING A *BREAK* FROM HIS EXPERIMENTS, RAY AND HIS LAWYER GIRLFRIEND *JEAN LORING* TOOK A GROUP OF STUDENTS TO EXPLORE A NEARBY *CAVERN*--

--WHERE THEY WERE ALL HOPELESSLY *TRAPPED* BY A SUDDEN *CAVE-IN*...

RAY REALIZED HIS ONLY HOPE OF *SAVING* JEAN AND THE KIDS MEANT USING HIS SPECIAL LENS ON *HIMSELF*, EVEN AT THE RISK OF HIS *LIFE*--

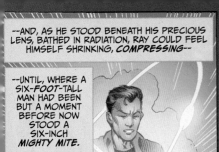

--AND, AS HE STOOD BENEATH HIS PRECIOUS LENS, BATHED IN RADIATION, RAY COULD FEEL HIMSELF SHRINKING, *COMPRESSING*--

DISCOVERING THAT HE MAINTAINED HIS NORMAL *STRENGTH* WHILE IN THIS TINY FORM, RAY TORE OPEN AN *ESCAPE ROUTE* FOR THE OTHERS, THEN BRACED HIMSELF FOR THE *INEVITABLE*--

--BUT, TO RAY'S *RELIEF* AND *ASTONISHMENT*, HE DID *NOT* EXPLODE.

--UNTIL, WHERE A SIX-*FOOT*-TALL MAN HAD BEEN BUT A MOMENT BEFORE NOW STOOD A SIX-INCH *MIGHTY MITE.*

FINDING THAT HE WAS SOME-HOW UNIQUELY *IMMUNE* TO THE LENS'S SIDE EFFECTS, RAY FASHIONED A COSTUME FROM *FIBERS* OF THE METEOR--

--AN OUTFIT THAT, REMARKABLY, BECAME *INVISIBLE* AND *INTANGIBLE* WHEN STRETCHED TO NORMAL SIZE--

--AND, NOW ABLE TO *CONTROL* HIS SIZE AND WEIGHT, PHYSICIST RAY PALMER BEGAN A WHOLE *NEW LIFE*--

--AS THE CRIME-FIGHTING *TINY TITAN* THE WORLD WOULD COME TO CALL-- *THE ATOM!*

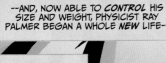

POWERS AND WEAPONS:

BY MANIPULATING HIDDEN CONTROLS IN HIS COSTUME, RAY PALMER CAN ADJUST HIS SIZE AND WEIGHT, ALLOWING HIM TO FLOAT ON AIR CURRENTS OR STRIKE WITH THE FORCE OF A FULL-SIZED MAN, DEPENDING ON HIS NEED. BECAUSE OF AN UNKNOWN FACTOR IN ITS MAKEUP, HIS COSTUME ORIGINALLY REMAINED BOTH INTANGIBLE AND INVISIBLE AT PALMER'S SIX-FOOT SIZE NOW AFTER RAY'S TRAVELS IN THE MULTIVERSE, HIS COSTUME CAN APPEAR WHEN HE GROWS TO NORMAL SIZE.

ALLIANCES:

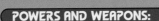

- JUSTICE LEAGUE OF AMERICA

ESSENTIAL STORYLINES:

- SHOWCASE PRESENTS THE ATOM
- IDENTITY CRISIS
- COUNTDOWN VOLUMES 1-4
- JUSTICE LEAGUE: CRY FOR JUSTICE

THE ORIGIN OF BANE

WRITER--SCOTT BEATTY
ARTIST--GRAHAM NOLAN
LETTERER--TRAVIS LANHAM
COLORIST--HI-FI
EDITOR--ELISABETH V. GEHRLEIN
BANE CREATED BY CHUCK DIXON,
DOUG MOENCH AND GRAHAM NOLAN

They say there is no such thing as original sin.

In Santa Prisca, a male child must suffer the sins of his father.

For the crimes of Sir Edmund Dorrance, the terrorist King Snake, I was born guilty, my inheritance a life sentence without reprieve.

In Pena Duro, even the most terrible men are easily worn down and broken.

To survive the "hard stone," one must have the will to become harder.

The hardest are banished to the Cavidad Obscura, a cell below sea level which floods each night at high tide.

From days to weeks and then months into ten long years, I escaped through meditation.

And when I was finally released from my pit, I set about improving myself.

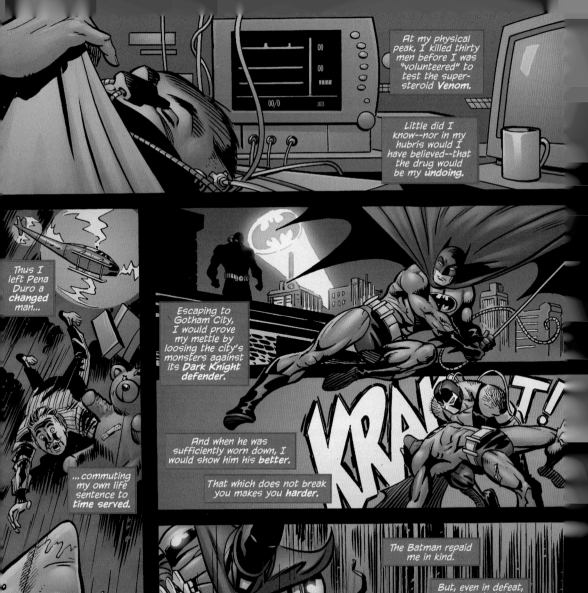

At my physical peak, I killed thirty men before I was "volunteered" to test the super-steroid Venom.

Little did I know--nor in my hubris would I have believed--that the drug would be my undoing.

Thus I left Pena Duro a changed man...

...commuting my own life sentence to time served.

Escaping to Gotham City, I would prove my mettle by loosing the city's monsters against its Dark Knight defender.

And when he was sufficiently worn down, I would show him his better.

That which does not break you makes you harder.

KRAKT!

The Batman repaid me in kind.

But, even in defeat, I achieved what no other has done nor will likely repeat...

I broke The Bat.

POWERS AND WEAPONS:

In Pena Duro, Bane came to believe that knowledge held true power. A voracious reader, he mastered six languages and studied philosophy and military strategy. Meditation furthered his mental growth, while a vigorous exercise regimen forged his body into a lethal weapon. The adrenocortico steroid Venom increased his strength and stamina tenfold. Bane beat his Venom addiction after the "replacement" Batman, Jean Paul Valley (A.K.A. Azrael), beat him into a coma. Upon waking, the withered Bane rebuilt his broken body to new levels of physical perfection.

ESSENTIAL STORYLINES:

- Batman: Knightfall Volumes 1-3
- Batman: Vengeance of Bane
- Batman: Vengeance of Bane II: The Redemption
- Batman: Bane
- Gotham Knights 33, 47-49

AFFILIATIONS:

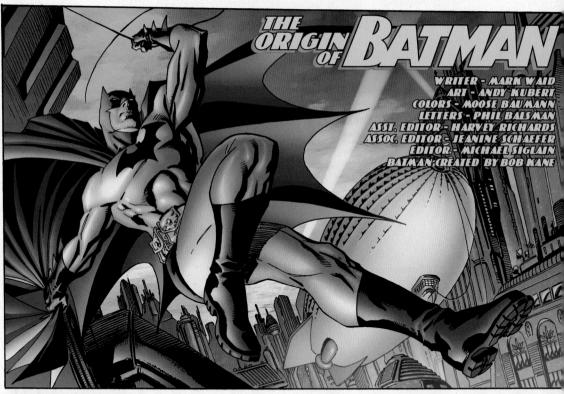

THE ORIGIN OF BATMAN

WRITER - MARK WAID
ART - ANDY KUBERT
COLORS - MOOSE BAUMANN
LETTERS - PHIL BALSMAN
ASST. EDITOR - HARVEY RICHARDS
ASSOC. EDITOR - JEANINE SCHAEFER
EDITOR - MICHAEL SIGLAIN
BATMAN CREATED BY BOB KANE

BRUCE WAYNE LEARNED THE POWER OF FEAR AS A BOY--

--WATCHING IN FROZEN HORROR AS HIS PARENTS, TWO OF GOTHAM CITY'S LEADING CITIZENS, WERE ROBBED AND MURDERED BY A COMMON THUG.

AT THEIR GRAVES, BRUCE SWORE A SOLEMN VOW TO AVENGE THEIR DEATHS.

RELYING LESS UPON HIS BILLION-DOLLAR INHERITANCE THAN ON HIS IRON WILL, BRUCE TRAVELED THE GLOBE--

--GRADUALLY TRAINING HIS MIND AND BODY TO THE PEAK OF HUMAN PERFECTION--

--WHILE STUDYING UNDER THE BEST CRIMINOLOGISTS, DETECTIVES AND FIGHTERS THE WORLD HAD TO OFFER.

RETURNING HOME, BRUCE TOOK TO THE STREETS AS A VIGILANTE CRIMEFIGHTER. DESPITE HIS SKILLS, HOWEVER, HE LACKED AN EDGE, A PRESENCE--

--UNTIL A STARTLING OMEN REMINDED HIM OF THE LESSON HE'D LEARNED THE NIGHT HIS PARENTS DIED.

TO BE TRULY EFFECTIVE, HE WOULD NEED MORE THAN GADGETS AND RESOURCES.

HE WOULD HAVE TO BECOME A CREATURE OF THE NIGHT--DARK, FRIGHTENING--

--ABLE TO STRIKE TERROR INTO THE HEARTS OF CRIMINALS.

AS A CHILD, FEAR WAS HIS WEAKNESS.

AS A MAN, IT BECAME HIS WEAPON.

POWERS AND WEAPONS:

Besides being a master of fighting styles, the Batman is a legendary escape artist and the world's greatest detective. His utility belt is stocked with a wide array of tools and armaments, including batarangs, grapnels and zip-lines, gas and smoke capsules, and remote controls for his fleet of Batmobiles.

ESSENTIAL STORYLINES:

THE BATMAN CHRONICLES
BATMAN: YEAR ONE
THE DARK KNIGHT RETURNS
BATMAN: THE GREATEST STORIES EVER TOLD

ALLIANCES:

Justice League of America

THE ORIGIN OF BEAST BOY

LEN WEIN · WRITER · RAFAEL ALBUQUERQUE · ART & COLOR
SAL CIPRIANO · LETTERS · ADAM SCHLAGMAN · EDITOR
BEAST BOY CREATED BY ARNOLD DRAKE

CHARLES DARWIN WOULD HAVE *HATED* GAR LOGAN...

GAR'S PARENTS, *MARK* AND *MARIE*, WERE SCIENTISTS, LIVING IN WEST AFRICA, STRIVING TO DISCOVER HOW TO *REVERSE EVOLUTION*--

--UNTIL THE DAY YOUNG GARFIELD CONTRACTED THE RARE BUT ALWAYS *FATAL* TROPICAL ILLNESS CALLED *SAKUTIA*...

KNOWING THAT ONLY THE LOCAL *GREEN MONKEY* HAD EVER *SURVIVED* THE DISEASE, GAR'S FATHER SUBJECTED HIM TO AN *EXPERIMENTAL RAY TREATMENT*--

--THAT, REMARKABLY, MOVED GAR *BACK* THROUGH THE EVOLUTIONARY CHAIN UNTIL HE LITERALLY *BECAME* THE MONKEY THAT COULD OVERCOME THE SICKNESS...

WHEN GAR FINALLY *RECOVERED*, THE ONLY LINGERING *AFTEREFFECT* WAS THAT HIS SKIN HAD NOW TURNED PERMANENTLY *GREEN*...

OR SO THEY THOUGHT...

WHEN HIS MOTHER'S *LIFE* WAS THREATENED, GAR DISCOVERED THAT HE COULD NOW *TRANSFORM* HIMSELF INTO ANY OTHER *LIVING CREATURE*--

--AN ABILITY THAT *SAVED HIS LIFE* AGAIN MONTHS LATER WHEN HIS PARENTS WERE WASHED TO THEIR *DEATHS* BY A SUDDEN *FLOOD*--

--LEAVING GAR AN *ORPHAN*...

SENT TO LIVE WITH HIS UNSCRUPULOUS UNCLE *SIMON GALTRY*, GAR EVENTUALLY *RAN AWAY*--

--AND SOON FOUND HIMSELF INVOLVED WITH THE *WORLD'S STRANGEST HEROES*, THE LEGENDARY *DOOM PATROL*...

...WHICH, IN TURN, LED TO GARFIELD LOGAN'S BECOMING ONE OF THE CHARTER MEMBERS OF THE *NEW TEEN TITANS*.

MAN, TALK ABOUT *EVOLUTION IN ACTION*...

POWERS AND WEAPONS:

BEAST BOY IS ABLE TO ASSUME THE SIZE, SHAPE, AND ABILITIES OF ANY ANIMAL HE CAN THINK OF, FROM A MICROBE TO A DINOSAUR TO A HUMMINGBIRD TO A LION--YOU NAME IT. HOWEVER, HE MUST REMAIN CONSCIOUS TO MAINTAIN THE ANIMAL FORM.

ALLIANCES:

- THE DOOM PATROL
- THE TEEN TITANS
- THE TITANS

ESSENTIAL STORYLINES:

- TEEN TITANS: BEAST BOYS & GIRLS
- THE NEW TEEN TITANS ARCHIVES VOL. 1-4
- NEW TEEN TITANS: TERRA INCOGNITO
- NEW TEEN TITANS: THE JUDAS CONTRACT
- TEEN TITANS: A KID'S GAME

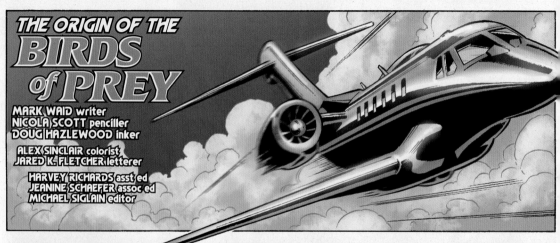

THE ORIGIN OF THE BIRDS of PREY

MARK WAID writer
NICOLA SCOTT penciller
DOUG HAZLEWOOD inker

ALEX SINCLAIR colorist
JARED K. FLETCHER letterer

HARVEY RICHARDS asst ed
JEANINE SCHAEFER assoc ed
MICHAEL SIGLAIN editor

BARBARA GORDON. BATGIRL. ONE OF THE DARK KNIGHT'S MOST TRUSTED ALLIES. A LITHE AND AGILE CRIMEFIGHTER--

--UNTIL THE JOKER'S GUN LEFT HER PARALYZED FOR LIFE.

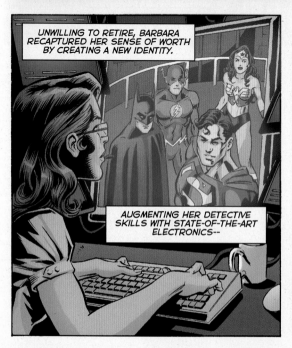

UNWILLING TO RETIRE, BARBARA RECAPTURED HER SENSE OF WORTH BY CREATING A NEW IDENTITY.

AUGMENTING HER DETECTIVE SKILLS WITH STATE-OF-THE-ART ELECTRONICS--

--SHE CREATED A NEW ALTER EGO AS THE ULTIMATE INFORMATION RESOURCE TO THE SUPER-HERO COMMUNITY.

BEFORE LONG, EVEN THOSE FEW WHO KNEW HER REAL NAME BEGAN THINKING OF HER ONLY BY HER NEW IDENTITY:

ORACLE.

ORACLE LEARNED THE ROPES OF ESPIONAGE AS AN ALLY OF THE SUICIDE SQUAD BEFORE STARTING HER OWN INTERNATIONAL CRIMEBUSTING OPERATION-- THE BIRDS OF PREY.

ORACLE'S NEXT AGENT WAS BLACK CANARY, AND THE TWO SLOWLY BECAME THE BEST OF FRIENDS. CANARY'S TOUR OF DUTY DEFINED THE TEAM AND ITS METHODS OF OPERATION--

HER FIRST AGENT, POWER GIRL, LEFT THE TEAM WHEN A MISSION WENT AWRY AND INNOCENT PEOPLE WERE KILLED-- SOMETHING THAT STRAINS THEIR RELATIONSHIP TO THIS DAY.

--GIVING IT THE LONG-TERM CREDIBILITY IT WOULD NEED TO OUTLAST HER ONCE SHE FINALLY LEFT THE GROUP.

ORIGINALLY BASED INSIDE A CLOCK TOWER IN GOTHAM, THE BIRDS NOW OPERATE FROM THE TOP FLOORS OF THE DALTEN TOWERS IN THE SHADOW OF METROPOLIS'S DAILY PLANET BUILDING--

--FLYING TO MISSIONS VIA THE AERIE ONE CESSNA AND THE AERIE TWO HELICOPTER, BOTH SPECIALLY MODIFIED BY THE LATE TED KORD.

NO ONE OPERATIVE COULD REPLACE CANARY. INSTEAD, ORACLE NOW RECRUITS ALLIES LARGELY ON AN AS-NEEDED BASIS-- SOME REGULARLY, OTHERS ONLY WHEN THEIR SPECIFIC SKILLS ARE REQUIRED. AMONG HER CORE OPERATIVES:

BIG BARDA
A super-strong New God.

MANHUNTER
A relentless fighter with a fierce thirst for justice.

LADY BLACKHAWK
A time-displaced pilot and markswoman.

HUNTRESS
The team's field leader.

ESSENTIAL STORYLINES:

Birds of Prey (2002)
BIRDS OF PREY: Of Like Minds
BIRDS OF PREY: The Battle Within
BIRDS OF PREY: Perfect Pitch

HELLO! ME NOT SEE YOU AGAIN!

"...BIZARRO LIVE UNHAPPILY EVER BEFORE!"

THIS MAKE BACK PAGE OF DALI PLANIT!

CHEESE!

POWERS AND WEAPONS:

Bizarro unlike Superman in every way except for superstrength and power to fly. Bizarro have ice-vision and flame-breath, minus "Bizarro Vision," imperfect duplicator rays which not create fewer Bizarros. Him also less handsome. But not everyone have chiseled bad looks!

ESSENTIAL STORYLINES:

- SUPERMAN: THE MAN OF STEEL VOLUME 1
- SUPERMAN: BIZARRO'S WORLD
- BIZARRO WORLD
- BIZARRO COMICS
- SUPERMAN/BATMAN: VENGEANCE
- SUPERMAN: EMPEROR JOKER
- SUPERMAN: ESCAPE FROM BIZARRO WORLD

"THERE, HIM DO BAD DEEDS. AND SO, SURROUNDED BY ALL HIM ENEMIES..."

OKAY! ME GOING, LOIS!

BIZARRO, NO SAVE ME!

"BIZARRO JOB TO DESTROY TERRIBLE MUTROPLIS CITY AS IT WORSTEST VILLAIN."

NO COME MUTROPLIS GO WAY!

NOT HOME OF BIZARRO! UH-UH!

"UNLUCKY THING BIZARRO WORLD NOT STILL AROUND TO SOAK UP RAYS OF UGLY BLUE SUN."

"IT NOT CALLED HTRAE, BY THE WAY."

THE ORIGIN OF BLACK ADAM

MARK WAID Writer • **JG JONES** Art
ALEX SINCLAIR Color • NICK J. NAPOLITANO Letters
STEPHEN WACKER & HARVEY RICHARDS Editors

IN THE 13TH CENTURY B.C., TETH-ADAM'S HEROIC DEEDS IN THE LAND OF KAHNDAQ EARNED HIM THE FAVOR OF THE WIZARD SHAZAM.

BY SPEAKING THE WIZARD'S NAME, TETH-ADAM WAS IMBUED WITH THE POWERS OF THE EGYPTIAN GODS AND SERVED AS THE MIGHTIEST WARRIOR OF PHARAOH RAMESES II.

UNFORTUNATELY, SHAZAM REALIZED TOO LATE THAT HE HAD RECRUITED A CHAMPION WITH A DARK TEMPER AND A DANGEROUSLY LIMITED DEFINITION OF JUSTICE.

WHEN HIS HOMELAND, WIFE AND CHILDREN WERE DESTROYED BY INVADING FORCES, ADAM'S THIRST FOR VENGEANCE DROVE HIM TO VIOLENTLY SEIZE THE THRONE OF KAHNDAQ AND RULE THE KINGDOM WITH AN IRON FIST.

BELIEVING THAT HIS STUDENT HAD BECOME IRREVOCABLY CORRUPT, SHAZAM RENAMED HIM "KHEM-ADAM" ("BLACK ADAM") AND BANISHED HIS SOUL INTO A MYSTIC SCARAB RATHER THAN ALLOW HIM THE FREEDOM TO MENACE EARTH UNCHECKED.

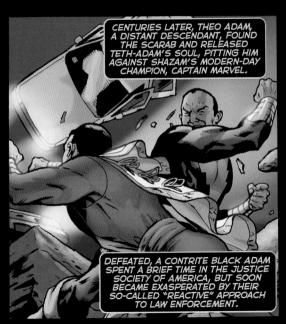

CENTURIES LATER, THEO ADAM, A DISTANT DESCENDANT, FOUND THE SCARAB AND RELEASED TETH-ADAM'S SOUL, PITTING HIM AGAINST SHAZAM'S MODERN-DAY CHAMPION, CAPTAIN MARVEL.

DEFEATED, A CONTRITE BLACK ADAM SPENT A BRIEF TIME IN THE JUSTICE SOCIETY OF AMERICA, BUT SOON BECAME EXASPERATED BY THEIR SO-CALLED "REACTIVE" APPROACH TO LAW ENFORCEMENT.

EVENTUALLY, ADAM RETURNED TO HIS ROOTS, TAKING KAHNDAQ BY FORCE ONCE AGAIN AND REESTABLISHING HIS "EYE FOR AN EYE" BRAND OF JUSTICE THROUGH BLOODY RETRIBUTION.

AS THE LEADER OF A SOVEREIGN NATION, HE IS BOTH FEARED AND WORSHIPPED. DESPITE HIS RAGE, HE SEES HIMSELF AS A HERO, HAVING VOWED TO PROTECT KAHNDAQ FROM ANY AND ALL WHO DARE THREATEN ITS BORDERS.

POWERS AND WEAPONS:

Possessing the abilities of six Egyptian gods--
*S*hu (god of stamina)
*H*eru (god of swiftness)
*A*mon (god of strength)
*Z*ehuti (god of wisdom)
*A*ton (god of power) and
*M*ehen (god of courage)
--Black Adam has super-strength, super-speed, a keen mind, and the power to fly.
He is virtually indestructible.

ESSENTIAL STORYLINES:

- The Power of Shazam!
- JSA: Black Reign
- Villains United
- 52

THE ORIGIN OF BLACK CANARY

Not many super-hero careers are motivated by a need to annoy your mom.

Mark Waid-Writer
Howard Chaykin-Artist
Pete Pantazis-Colors
Nick Napolitano-Letters
Harvey Richards-Asst. Ed.
Jeanine Schaefer-Assoc. Ed
Michael Siglain-Editor

Then again, Dinah Lance always enjoyed breaking rules.

Dinah's mother was the original Black Canary, one of the world's first crimefighting heroines--

--and one who actively discouraged her daughter from braving such a risk-filled life.

Luckily, Dinah's "uncles" in the Justice Society--realizing where Dinah's rebelliousness would take her--trained her in secret, not only in martial arts--

--but in the use of her own unique meta-human power, a piercing ultrasonic scream that can shatter solid objects and disorient opponents.

Defying her mother's wishes, Dinah assumed the Black Canary identity and the blonde bombshell lifestyle like a blossoming flower, embracing both with a fierce and joyful gusto.

Canary is both a solo act and a dependable team player. Having served with the Justice League and the Justice Society--

--her closest friends are the Birds of Prey, a network of female agents overseen by the cyberoperative Oracle.

POWERS AND WEAPONS:

Besides being a skilled martial artist and motorcyclist, Black Canary can pulverize small objects (and eardrums) with her ultrasonic scream.

ESSENTIAL STORYLINES:

• Black Canary/Oracle: Birds of Prey
• Birds of Prey: Of Like Minds
• Secret Origins 50

ALLIANCES:

Justice League, Birds of Prey

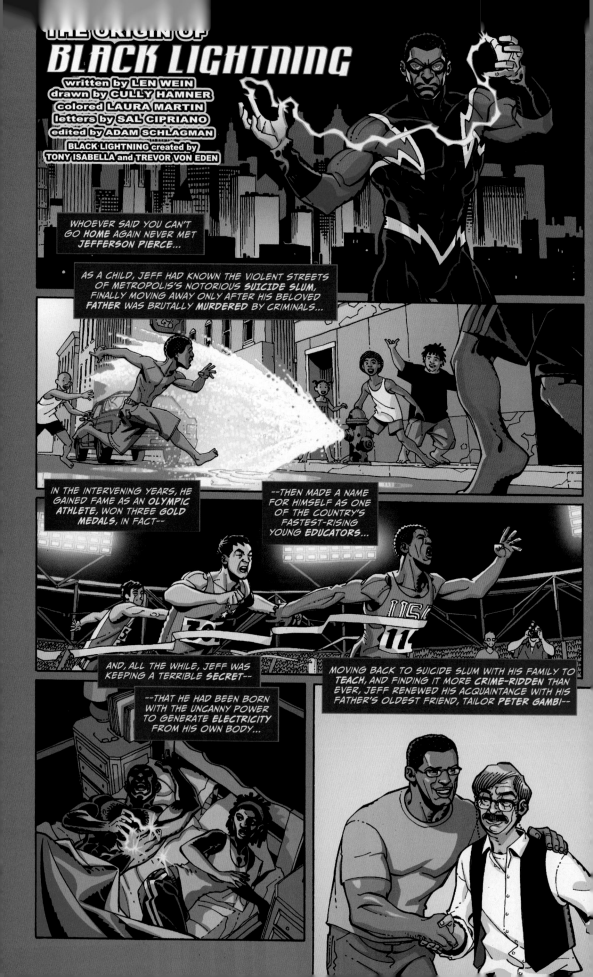

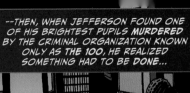

--THEN, WHEN JEFFERSON FOUND ONE OF HIS BRIGHTEST PUPILS *MURDERED* BY THE CRIMINAL ORGANIZATION KNOWN ONLY AS *THE 100*, HE REALIZED SOMETHING HAD TO BE *DONE*...

AT JEFFERSON'S REQUEST, PETER GAMBI USED HIS OWN NOT-INCONSIDERABLE SKILLS TO DESIGN A *COSTUME* THAT COULD *HARNESS* JEFFERSON'S ELECTRICAL ABILITIES--

--AND, DETERMINED TO LIVE BY HIS FATHER'S FAVORITE *MOTTO*, THAT "JUSTICE--LIKE LIGHTNING--SHOULD EVER APPEAR TO SOME MEN HOPE, TO OTHER MEN, FEAR"--

--*BLACK LIGHTNING* TOOK TO THE STREETS TO *RECLAIM* SUICIDE SLUM FROM GANG BOSS TOBIAS WHALE AND THE EVIL OF *THE 100*.

POWERS AND WEAPONS:

Black Lightning is an Olympic-level athlete and gymnast, whose body generates a powerful electrical current that is harnessed and channeled through hidden circuitry in his costume. He can wield this energy as electrical blasts or focus it into a protective forcefield with limited range.

ALLIANCES:

- Justice League of America
- The Outsiders

ESSENTIAL STORYLINES:

- Black Lightning Year One

THE ORIGIN OF BLACK MANTA

writer–SCOTT BEATTY
penciller–MIKE NORTON
inker–RODNEY RAMOS
letterer–KEN LOPEZ
colorist–HI-FI
editor–ELISABETH U. GEHRLEIN

THE HIGH SEAS HAVE A LONG AND STORIED HISTORY OF *PIRACY*.

IN MODERN TIMES, THE SO-CALLED *BLACK MANTA* LAID CLAIM TO THE OCEANS' BOUNTY OF SUNKEN TREASURE AND OTHER RICHES.

SWIMMING IN THE WAY OF BLACK MANTA'S PLUNDERING AND PILLAGING WAS THE KING OF THE SEVEN SEAS, WHO HAD LITTLE PATIENCE FOR SURFACE MEN WITH PLANS TO SACK THE SUNKEN CITY OF ATLANTIS.

AND SO IT WENT FOR YEARS, AQUAMAN DROWNING ALL OF BLACK MANTA'S AQUATIC AMBITIONS...

...UNTIL THE VILLAIN MADE THEIR CONFLICT *PERSONAL*.

FOR KILLING HIS SON BY SUFFOCATING HIM IN A SPHERE FILLED WITH AIR INSTEAD OF WATER, A GRIEF-STRICKEN AQUAMAN SQUEEZED BLACK MANTA'S REBREATHER TUBES SHUT TO END HIS VILLAINY FOREVER.

BUT BLACK MANTA BEGGED FOR THE KIND OF *MERCY* ONLY A KING COULD GRANT.

AND WHEN THEIR CONFLICT CONTINUED AS BEFORE, BLACK MANTA BESEECHED THE DEVILISH *NERON* TO TURN THE TIDE IN *HIS* FAVOR.

TRANSFORMED INTO A *TRUE* UNDERSEA CREATURE BEFITTING HIS NAMESAKE, BLACK MANTA SANK TO NEW DEPTHS OF DEPRAVITY...

...UNTIL AQUAMAN, ONCE MORE GRANTING MERCY, FISHED OUT BLACK MANTA'S SUBMERGED HUMANITY...

...AND RESTORED THE VILLAIN TO NORMAL WITH A HEALING HAND.

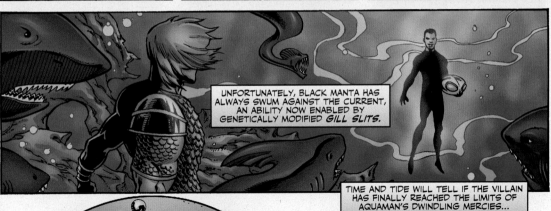

UNFORTUNATELY, BLACK MANTA HAS ALWAYS SWUM AGAINST THE CURRENT, AN ABILITY NOW ENABLED BY GENETICALLY MODIFIED *GILL SLITS*.

TIME AND TIDE WILL TELL IF THE VILLAIN HAS FINALLY REACHED THE LIMITS OF AQUAMAN'S DWINDLING MERCIES...

...OR IF BLACK MANTA PLANS A WHOLE NEW WAVE OF MARITIME MAYHEM!

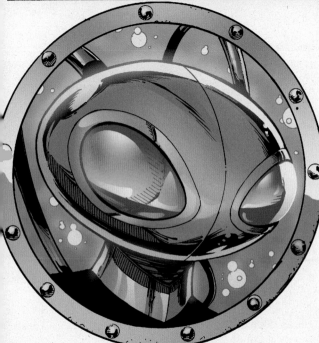

POWERS AND WEAPONS:

Previously, Black Manta had no special powers, but instead relied on his specialized diving suit to provide breathable air and protection from both temperature extremes and crushing pressures in the deepest waters. The lenses of Black Manta's helmet emit destructive laser beams. Having spent so much time underwater, he has become a skilled and deadly undersea combatant. Black Manta's Manta-Ship is a stealthy, swift, and heavily armed submersible vehicle. In addition, Black Manta sometimes employs loyal "Manta-Men" henchmen who have undergone gill-implantation to breathe underwater. A similar procedure now enables Black Manta to do the same.

ESSENTIAL STORYLINES:

- AQUAMAN 35 (vol 1)
- ADVENTURE COMICS 452
- AQUAMAN 57 (vol 1)
- AQUAMAN 29-30 (vol 3)
- AQUAMAN 8, 39 (vol 4)

AFFILIATIONS:

- O.G.R.E. (Organization for General Revenge and Enslavement)
- Injustice League of America

THE ORIGIN OF BLUE BEETLE

WRITER-MARK WAID
ARTIST-CULLY HAMNER
COLORIST-ALEX SINCLAIR
LETTERER-TRAVIS LANHAM
ASST ED-HARVEY RICHARDS
ASSOC ED-JEANINE SCHAEFER
EDITORS-WACKER & SIGLAIN

FROM THE ROCK OF ETERNITY TO A VACANT LOT IN EL PASO, TEXAS. AN IGNOMINIOUS JOURNEY FOR THE FABLED MYSTIC SCARAB OF THE BLUE BEETLE.

THE MAGICIANS OF THE UNIVERSE HAD WRITTEN IT OFF. THEY'D MISTAKEN DORMANCY...

...FOR POWERLESSNESS. BUT WHEN TEENAGER JAIME REYES STUMBLED ACROSS IT BY CHANCE, SOMETHING CHITTERY IN THE SCARAB AWOKE...

...AND, IN THE NIGHT, FOUND A NEW SYMBIOTIC HOST BY FUSING TO JAIME'S SPINE.

JAIME AWOKE BABBLING ALIEN LANGUAGES AND HEARING AND SEEING UNINTELLIGIBLE COMMUNICATIONS FROM THE SCARAB.

IT WAS TRYING--AND FAILING MISERABLY--TO WARN JAIME THAT, WHENEVER HE FACED DANGER, THE SCARAB WOULD EXPAND TO CREATE A SUPER-POWERED CARAPACE AROUND HIS BODY.

AT FIRST, THESE CHANGES LEFT THE BOY FRIGHTENED AND VICTIMIZED--

--BUT BEFORE FEAR COULD FOREVER CRIPPLE HIM, HE WAS DRAFTED INTO SERVICE ALONGSIDE EARTH'S DEFENDERS TO DEFEAT THE OMNISCIENT BROTHER EYE--

--A MISSION THAT FAST-TRACKED JAIME TOWARD A HEROIC DESTINY.

NOW, AS BLUE BEETLE, JAIME (IN BETWEEN CLASSES) PROTECTS EL PASO FROM A WIDE ARRAY OF CRIMINAL AND MAGICAL THREATS...

...ALL THE WHILE TRYING TO SOLVE THE MYSTERIES OF WHO CREATED THE SCARAB...AND WHEN THEY'RE COMING BACK.

BELLS CARGO

POWERS AND WEAPONS:

The Beetle armor can reconfigure to create energy cannons, blades and shields, and wings which give Blue Beetle the power of flight. Its A.I. weapons system allows Beetle to lock onto and track any energy source--biological, technological, or mystical.

ESSENTIAL STORYLINES:

- Infinite Crisis
- Blue Beetle 7
- Blue Beetle: Shellshocked

The Origin of BOO$TER GOLD

MARK WAID - writer
DAN JURGENS - penciller
ANDY LANNING - inker
ALEX SINCLAIR - colorist
PAT BROSSEAU - letterer
HARVEY RICHARDS - asst. editor
STEPHEN WACKER - editor
BOOSTER GOLD created by
DAN JURGENS

MICHAEL JON "BOOSTER" CARTER-- SUPERSTAR QUARTERBACK AND GOTHAM UNIVERSITY M.V.P. TWO YEARS RUNNING: (2461 AND 2462). GOTHAM'S FAVORITE SON--

--UNTIL HE WAS CAUGHT BETTING ON HIS OWN GAMES.

THE BRIGHTEST STARS BURN THE FASTEST. BOOSTER'S SPORTS CAREER ENDED IN DISGRACE.

BANNED

HAVING NO OTHER SKILLS OR OPPORTUNITIES, BLOWING EVERY CHANCE AT REDEMPTION, BOOSTER EVENTUALLY ENDED UP A MENIAL NIGHT WATCHMAN AT THE "SPACE MUSEUM," THE 25TH CENTURY'S MEMORIAL TO HEROES PAST.

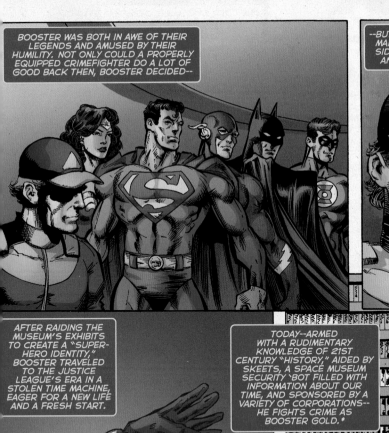

BOOSTER WAS BOTH IN AWE OF THEIR LEGENDS AND AMUSED BY THEIR HUMILITY. NOT ONLY COULD A PROPERLY EQUIPPED CRIMEFIGHTER DO A LOT OF GOOD BACK THEN, BOOSTER DECIDED--

--BUT A SMART ONE COULD MAKE A KILLING ON THE SIDE IN MERCHANDISING AND ENDORSEMENTS.

AFTER RAIDING THE MUSEUM'S EXHIBITS TO CREATE A "SUPER-HERO IDENTITY," BOOSTER TRAVELED TO THE JUSTICE LEAGUE'S ERA IN A STOLEN TIME MACHINE, EAGER FOR A NEW LIFE AND A FRESH START.

TODAY--ARMED WITH A RUDIMENTARY KNOWLEDGE OF 21ST CENTURY "HISTORY," AIDED BY SKEETS, A SPACE MUSEUM SECURITY 'BOT FILLED WITH INFORMATION ABOUT OUR TIME, AND SPONSORED BY A VARIETY OF CORPORATIONS-- HE FIGHTS CRIME AS BOOSTER GOLD.*

*GRATUITY NOT INCLUDED.

POWERS AND WEAPONS:

Booster's augmented suit gives him super-strength and protects him with force-fields. His gauntlets emit destructive energy beams while his stolen ring allows him to fly.

His companion, Skeets, possesses no combat capabilities but can act independently and flies under his own power.

ESSENTIAL STORYLINES:

- BOOSTER GOLD: 52 PICK-UP
- FORMERLY KNOWN AS THE JUSTICE LEAGUE
- COUNTDOWN TO INFINITE CRISIS
- THE OMAC PROJECT
- 52

ALLIANCES:

Justice League of America

THE ORIGIN OF Captain MARVEL

LEN WEIN WRITER   SHANE DAVIS PENCILLER
SANDRA HOPE INKER   ALEX SINCLAIR COLORS
SWANDS LETTERS   ADAM SCHLAGMAN EDITOR

IT WAS A VERY *DIFFERENT* WORLD IN THOSE DAYS...

ONE COLD RAINY NIGHT, ORPHANED NEWSBOY *BILLY BATSON* WAS APPROACHED BY A MYSTERIOUS *STRANGER*, WHO SAID TO HIM:

FOLLOW ME!

AND, REMARKABLY, BILLY *DID.*

THE STRANGER LED BILLY TO A *CATACOMB* HIDDEN DEEP BENEATH THE *FAWCETT CITY SUBWAY SYSTEM*--

--WHERE A *SUBWAY CAR* OF MOST *SINGULAR* DESIGN SAT WAITING FOR HIM...

HAVE NO FEAR. EVERYTHING HAS BEEN ARRANGED.

THE TRAIN TOOK THE BOY TO A TIME-TOSSED UNDERGROUND *CAVERN*, GUARDED BY SEVEN LEGENDARY FIGURES--

--WHERE AN EVEN MORE *IMPOSING* FIGURE AWAITED HIM...

WELCOME, BILLY BATSON.

PRIDE   GREED

H-HOW DO YOU KNOW MY *NAME?*

I KNOW *EVERYTHING.*

I AM... SHAZAM!

SOLOMON WISDOM
HERCULES STRENGTH
ATLAS STAMINA
ZEUS POWER
ACHILLES COURAGE
MERCURY SPEED

FOR 3,000 YEARS, I HAVE USED MY GODS-GIVEN POWERS TO BATTLE THE FORCES OF *EVIL* WHICH THREATEN TO *EXTINGUISH* MAN FROM THE FACE OF THE EARTH.

BUT I AM *OLD* NOW, AND I HAVE CHOSEN *YOU* TO BE MY *SUCCESSOR.* WITH ONE WORD, YOU CAN BECOME THE *MIGHTIEST MAN* IN THE WORLD.

BILLY BATSON, SPEAK MY *NAME!*

SHAZAM!

THE WORD WAS SPOKEN, A BOLT OF *MYSTIC LIGHTNING* ARCED DOWN FROM THE HEAVENS, AND THE TIMID NEWSBOY WAS *GONE*...

IN HIS PLACE NOW STOOD THE *WORLD'S MIGHTIEST MORTAL*...

WELCOME... *CAPTAIN MARVEL.*

HENCEFORTH, IT SHALL BE YOUR DUTY TO *DEFEND* THE POOR AND HELPLESS, *RIGHT* WRONGS AND CRUSH *EVIL* EVERYWHERE.

DO YOU *ACCEPT* THIS SACRED HONOR?

I DO.

AND THUS ARE *LEGENDS* BORN...

Powers and Weapons:

GRANTED THE POWERS OF THE ANCIENT GODS, CAPTAIN MARVEL POSSESSES THE WISDOM OF SOLOMON, THE STRENGTH OF HERCULES, THE STAMINA OF ATLAS, THE POWER OF ZEUS, THE COURAGE OF ACHILLES, AND THE SPEED OF MERCURY, AS WELL AS INVULNERABILITY AND THE POWER OF FLIGHT. HIS NOBLE HEART IS HIS GREATEST WEAPON.

Essential Storylines:

· THE TRIALS OF SHAZAM
· JUSTICE SOCIETY OF AMERICA: BLACK ADAM AND ISIS
· THE POWER OF SHAZAM
· DAY OF VENGEANCE
· SUPERMAN/SHAZAM: FIRST THUNDER

AFFILIATIONS:

· JUSTICE SOCIETY OF AMERICA
· THE MARVEL FAMILY

CATMAN

WRITER - MARK WAID
PENCILLER - DALE EAGLESHAM
INKER- ART THIBERT
COLORIST - ALEX SINCLAIR
LETTERER - ROB LEIGH
ASST. ED. - HARVEY RICHARDS
ASSOC. ED. - JEANINE SCHAEFER
EDITORS - WACKER & SIGLAIN

BOREDOM IS THE WORST IMAGINABLE REASON FOR BECOMING A SUPER-VILLAIN IN GOTHAM CITY.

CLOAKED IN A MAGIC AFRICAN CLOTH THAT GAVE HIM NINE LIVES, BIG-GAME TRAPPER THOMAS BLAKE SOUGHT THRILLS BY HUNTING THE BATMAN.

NINE LIVES... AND "CATMAN" BECAME A JOKE IN ALL OF THEM.

DOWN AND OUT, FAT AND TIRED, BLAKE EARNED THE CONTEMPT OF HEROES AND VILLAINS ALIKE.

EVERY TIME HE HIT BOTTOM, HE FOUND SOME WAY TO KEEP DIGGING.

EVENTUALLY, POWERLESS AND DESPERATE TO REKINDLE HIS CONFIDENCE, BLAKE RETURNED TO THE JUNGLES OF AFRICA...

...AND FOUND HIS PRIDE ONCE MORE.

LIVING AMONG THE JUNGLE CATS, BONDING WITH THEM, BLAKE REGAINED HIS SELF-ESTEEM AND FIGHTING SKILLS.

--BUT LEX LUTHOR HAD OTHER PLANS FOR HIM. AT LUTHOR'S DIRECTION, THE ENTIRE PRIDE WAS SLAUGHTERED--

HE WOULD GLADLY HAVE SPENT THE REST OF TIME ALONGSIDE HIS NEW BROTHERS--

--SPURRING AN ENRAGED BLAKE INTO RECLAIMING HIS COSTUMED IDENTITY TO HUNT THEIR KILLER. THIS, TOO, WAS PART OF LUTHOR'S PLAN--

--BUT IT BACKFIRED WHEN CATMAN, ALLIED WITH THE CRIMINAL SYNDICATE KNOWN AS THE SECRET SIX, REFUSED TO PLAY LUTHOR'S GAMES.

DEADLIER THAN EVER BEFORE, CATMAN NOW HUNTS AND PUNISHES THOSE WHO HE BELIEVES ABUSE THEIR POWER... WHETHER HERO OR VILLAIN.

POWERS AND WEAPONS:

Catman is a fierce warrior who fights by the law of the jungle and is one of the greatest hunters and trackers alive.
He is particularly skilled in the use of bladed weapons and is uncannily stealthy and agile.

ESSENTIAL STORYLINES:

- DETECTIVE COMICS 311
- GREEN ARROW: THE ARCHER'S QUEST
- VILLAINS UNITED

ALLIANCES:

Secret Six

SOME WITCHES HAVE UNCOMMON *BEAUTY* THAT BELIES THEIR MORE *BEASTLY* NATURE.

THE ORIGIN OF CIRCE

WRITER--SCOTT BEATTY
ARTIST--AARON LOPRESTI
LETTERER--KEN LOPEZ
COLORIST--HI-FI
EDITOR--ELISABETH V. GEHRLEIN

FOR CENTURIES, THE SORCERESS CIRCE RULED THE ISLAND OF AEAEA ATTENDED BY HER ABOMINABLE *BESTIAMORPHS.*

LURED BY THE SIRENS' SONGS, COUNTLESS MEN DIED UPON THE JAGGED ROCKS SURROUNDING AEAEA.

BUT EVEN DEATH BY DROWNING WAS PREFERABLE TO A LIFE TRANSFORMED AS A *MONSTER* IN CIRCE'S THRALL.

HER THIRST FOR POWER *UNQUENCHABLE,* CIRCE FORGED A TERRIBLE PACT WITH THE WITCH-GODDESS *HECATE.*

THUS, CIRCE WAS REMADE IN A CRUCIBLE OF FIRE TO BECOME HECATE'S INSTRUMENT OF *VENGEANCE* AGAINST THE OLYMPIAN GODS WHO WRONGED HER.

PERHAPS, THEN, IT WAS FATED THAT CIRCE'S GREATEST FOE WOULD BE THE AMAZONIAN PRINCESS DIANA, WHOSE POWERS AS *WONDER WOMAN* WERE GIFTS FROM THE OLYMPIANS CIRCE HAD TRADED HER VERY SOUL TO *DESTROY.*

CIRCE LATER DONNED THE GLAMOUR OF ATTORNEY *DONNA MILTON* TO GET CLOSE ENOUGH TO WONDER WOMAN TO SLIT HER THROAT.

SO AS TO FOOL DIANA'S *LASSO OF TRUTH*, CIRCE BEWITCHED HERSELF TO BELIEVE THAT SHE TRULY *WAS* MILTON, AND WAS THEREFORE UNABLE TO RESIST THE CHARMS OF UNDERWORLD BOSS *ARES BUCHANAN*, THE OLYMPIAN GOD OF WAR SIMILARLY DISGUISED!

AFTER ARES CLAIMED YOUNG LYTA AS HIS OWN, THEN, PERHAPS IT WAS ALSO FATED THAT CIRCE WOULD USE HER WITCHY WILES ON A REBORN *HIPPOLYTA.*

BUT EVEN THE MOST *UNHOLY* UNIONS CAN PRODUCE THINGS OF BEAUTY.

CIRCE NAMED THEIR DAUGHTER *LYTA*, A NOT-SO-SUBTLE STAB AT WONDER WOMAN'S OWN BELOVED AND DEPARTED MOTHER, QUEEN HIPPOLYTA.

THUS COMPELLED, HIPPOLYTA ORDERED HER AMAZONS TO ATTACK MAN'S WORLD IN AN ALL-OUT *WAR.*

BY SPARKING THE NEAR-GENOCIDAL CONFLICT, CIRCE AIMED TO ROB THE GODS OF THEIR AMAZONIAN CHILDREN, BUT SHE WAS INSTEAD BANISHED TO *HADES* FOR THE ATTEMPT.

TIME WILL TELL WHICH BURNS *HOTTER*--

--THE HELLFIRES OF THE UNDERWORLD...

...OR CIRCE'S OWN SEARING *HATRED* FOR WONDER WOMAN!

POWERS AND WEAPONS:

Circe is an immortal sorceress of incalculable power. She is able to alter her own appearance, transform men into hybrid bestiamorphs, or cast mystical bolts of destructive energy from her fingertips. Her greatest power, however, is the ability to manipulate god, man, or beast into doing her evil bidding.

ESSENTIAL STORYLINES:

- WONDER WOMAN: BEAUTY AND THE BEASTS
- WONDER WOMAN: THE CHALLENGE OF ARTEMIS
- WONDER WOMAN: PARADISE FOUND
- WONDER WOMAN: WHO IS WONDER WOMAN?
- AMAZONS ATTACK

AFFLIATIONS:

THE INJUSTICE GANG

THE ORIGIN OF CONGORILLA

LEN WEIN—WRITER
ARDIAN SYAF—PENCILLER
JOHN DELL—INKER
PETE PANTAZIS—COLORS
SAL CIPRIANO—LETTERS
ADAM SCHLAGMAN—EDITOR

THERE WAS A REASON THEY USED TO CALL IT *DARKEST* AFRICA, LAND OF MYSTERY AND BOUNDLESS *SUPERSTITION...*

BUT TO THE LEGENDARY EXPLORER AND ADVENTURER KNOWN ONLY AS *CONGO BILL,* THE DARK CONTINENT WAS, QUITE SIMPLY, *HOME—*

--AND HE WAS SWORN TO DO WHATEVER IT MIGHT TAKE TO *PROTECT* IT.

STILL, WHEN BILL WAS CALLED TO THE DEATHBED OF HIS OLD FRIEND *CHIEF KAWOLO,* AND OFFERED WHAT THE MEDICINE MAN CALLED A *MAGIC RING,* BILL WAS EXTREMELY *SKEPTICAL—*

--ESPECIALLY WHEN THE OLD MAN TOLD HIM THAT *RUBBING* THE RING WOULD ALLOW BILL TO *TRANSFER HIS MIND* INTO THE BODY OF THE LEGENDARY *GOLDEN GORILLA* OF THE VELDT.

TO *HUMOR* HIS DYING FRIEND, THOUGH, BILL *ACCEPTED* THE GIFT GRACIOUSLY—

--AND THAT SINGLE ACT OF SELFLESS GENEROSITY ULTIMATELY *SAVED* BILL'S LIFE.

SEVERAL WEEKS LATER, A SUDDEN EARTH TREMOR TRIGGERED A *LANDSLIDE* THAT LEFT BILL HOPELESSLY *TRAPPED* IN A REMOTE *CAVE...*

EXHAUSTING EVERY *OTHER* POSSIBLE MEANS OF ESCAPE, BILL REMEMBERED KAWOLO'S *GIFT*...

WITH NOTHING LEFT TO *LOSE*, BILL *RUBBED* THE RING--

--AND THE WORLD BLURRED INTO *MADNESS*.

INSTANTLY, DESPITE HIS EARLIER *DOUBTS*, BILL'S CONSCIOUSNESS FOUND ITSELF IN THE BODY OF THE *GOLDEN GORILLA*--

--NOW TOTALLY IN CONTROL OF ONE OF THE MOST *POWERFUL* CREATURES ALIVE.

RACING TO THE CAVE-IN, THE GOLDEN GORILLA USED HIS GREAT STRENGTH TO *CLEAR* THE BLOCKED ENTRANCE--

--ALL THE WHILE WONDERING WHAT HAD BECOME OF HIS *BODY* WHILE HE'D BEEN OUT--

--AND ULTIMATELY RELIEVED TO DISCOVER THAT THE *BANANA*, SO TO SPEAK, HADN'T FALLEN VERY FAR FROM THE *TREE*.

POWERS AND WEAPONS:

By rubbing a magic ring he wears, Congo Bill can trade minds with the legendary golden gorilla known as Congorilla. The gorilla is possessed of extraordinary strength, agility, and dexterity, a mighty weapon when wielded with a razor-sharp human intelligence.

ALLIANCES:

• The Forgotten Heroes
• Justice League

ESSENTIAL STORYLINES:

• More Fun Comics #56
• Action Comics #248
• Justice League: Cry For Justice

WITH VIC *MANGLED* ALMOST BEYOND RECOGNITION, SILAS SAW ONLY ONE WAY TO *SAVE* HIS PRECIOUS SON'S LIFE--

--OUTFITTING WHAT *REMAINED* OF VIC'S BODY WITH THE COMPONENTS OF AN UNTESTED *CYBERNETIC SUIT* SILAS HAD ALSO DESIGNED.

WHEN VICTOR FINALLY REGAINED *CONSCIOUSNESS* MORE THAN A MONTH LATER, HE WAS NOT *HAPPY* WITH THE RESULTS OF HIS FATHER'S EFFORTS...

WHAT HE SAW IN THE MIRROR WAS NOT AN *ATHLETE*, BUT RATHER A *MONSTER*.

IT TOOK A *YEAR* BEFORE VIC'S FATHER FULLY TAUGHT HIM HOW TO *USE* HIS NEW BODY, HIS NEW *ABILITIES*--

--AND MORE MONTHS STILL BEFORE VIC WAS WILLING TO GO OUT IN *PUBLIC*.

BUT WHEN, AT LAST, HE DID, VIC DISCOVERED A WHOLE *NEW* LIFE AS A FOUNDING MEMBER OF THE NEW *TEEN TITANS*...

...AND THE *CHAMPION* HE WAS ALWAYS MEANT TO BECOME!

POWERS AND WEAPONS:

The bulk of his body encased in a cybernetic suit designed for the military, Cyborg has enhanced strength, speed, and stamina. He carries an array of detachable sonic and laser weapons that can be used in place of his hands.

ALLIANCES:

∘ The Teen Titans
∘ The Titans

ESSENTIAL STORYLINES:

∘ DC Spotlight: Cyborg
∘ Teen Titans: A Kid's Game

CONSIDER HIM A MAN OF STEEL FORGED IN A BROKEN MOLD.

THE ORIGIN OF CYBORG SUPERMAN

WRITER--SCOTT BEATTY
PENCILLER--IVAN REIS
INKER--OCLAIR ALBERT
COLORIST--HI-FI
LETTERER--KEN LOPEZ
EDITOR--ELISABETH V. GEHRLEIN

SUPERMAN CREATED BY JERRY SIEGEL AND JOE SHUSTER

ASTRONAUT *HANK HENSHAW* AND THE CREW OF THE SPACE SHUTTLE EXCALIBUR WERE ILL-PREPARED FOR THE CASCADING SOLAR RADIATION THAT ALTERED THEIR BODIES AT THE CELLULAR LEVEL.

THEIR BODIES MUTATING, HENSHAW AND HIS WIFE TERRI, AS WELL AS LIFELONG FRIENDS JIM AND STEVE, CRASH-LANDED NEAR METROPOLIS.

UNFORTUNATELY, HENSHAW AND HIS FELLOW ASTRONAUTS WERE MISTAKEN FOR MONSTERS AND WASTED PRECIOUS TIME BATTLING SUPERMAN, WHO REALIZED TOO LATE THEIR *TRUE* IDENTITIES.

DESPITE DESPERATE ATTEMPTS AT *S.T.A.R. LABS* TO REVERSE THE TRANSFORMATIONS, HENSHAW DISINTEGRATED IN SUPERMAN'S ARMS, UNABLE TO RESTORE HIS BELOVED WIFE TERRI TO CORPOREAL FORM.

LITTLE DID THE MAN OF STEEL REALIZE THAT HENSHAW HAD TRANSITIONED TO A "HIGHER" STATE OF BEING.

ABLE TO INVADE ANY METAL AND RECONSTITUTE HIMSELF ONE ATOM AT A TIME, HENSHAW RETURNED TO LIFE ONLY TO DISCOVER THAT HE HAD SUCCEEDED IN TEMPORARILY SOLIDIFYING TERRI'S BODY, BUT NOT HER SPIRIT.

HENSHAW FLED EARTH WITH ALLOYS AND TRACE ORGANIC MATERIALS APPROPRIATED FROM THE ORBITING SPACECRAFT THAT HAD FERRIED THE INFANT SUPERMAN FROM DOOMED KRYPTON MANY YEARS BEFORE.

BLAMING SUPERMAN FOR HIS EVERY LOSS, HENSHAW FOUND AN EAGER ALLY IN THE ALIEN OVERLORD MONGUL.

FUELED BY HATE, HENSHAW REBUILT HIMSELF AGAIN AND MASQUERADED AS A CYBORG-SUPERMAN BENT ON DESTROYING THE *REAL* MAN OF STEEL.

THOUGH FAILING IN HIS FIRST ATTEMPT, THE CYBORG-SUPERMAN WOULD CONTINUE TO CONCEIVE ELABORATE STRATAGEMS IN THE COMPANY OF *OTHER* MONSTERS DESIRING THE DEATH OF SUPERMAN.

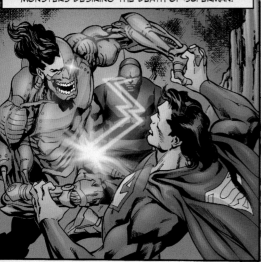

FOR HANK HENSHAW--NO MATTER WHAT GUISE HE WEARS--BELIEVES THAT IN FINALLY KILLING THE MAN OF STEEL, OR BY CONSORTING WITH BEINGS POWERFUL ENOUGH TO DO SO, HE MIGHT ALSO ACHIEVE THE ONE THING HE DESIRES FOR HIMSELF...

OBLIVION.

POWERS AND WEAPONS:

Able to mold and meld metals into new bodies for himself, the Cyborg-Superman is virtually immortal, as well as nearly invulnerable since absorbing the Kryptonian alloys from Kal-El's spacecraft. Armed with a Sinestro Corps ring on every metallic finger, the Cyborg-Superman was one of the most dangerous beings in the entire universe. His present whereabouts are unknown.

ESSENTIAL STORYLINES:

- WORLD WITHOUT A SUPERMAN
- SUPERMAN/DOOMSDAY: HUNTER/PREY
- GREEN LANTERN: THE SINESTRO CORPS WAR
- GREEN LANTERN: TALES OF THE SINESTRO CORPS

THE ORIGIN OF DARKSEID

WRITER--SCOTT BEATTY
ARTIST--RYAN SOOK
LETTERER--TRAVIS LANHAM
COLORIST--HI-FI
EDITOR--ELISABETH V. GEHRLEIN
DARKSEID CREATED BY JACK KIRBY

THERE CAME A TIME WHEN THE *OLD GODS* DIED...

THEIRS WAS A CONFLICT SO FIERCE, SO *FINAL*, A ONCE VIBRANT WORLD WAS TORN ASUNDER IN THE FIRST GREAT HOLOCAUST...

...A COSMIC CATACLYSM STILL RESOUNDING TO THE FAR CORNERS OF CREATION.

BUT NATURE ABHORS A VACUUM, AND THUS ONE BECAME *TWO*...

SPINNING 'ROUND ONE ANOTHER, ONE DARK, ONE LIGHT, BURNING APOKOLIPS AND VERDANT NEW GENESIS FILLED THE VOID, AND THE *NEW GODS* POPULATED PLANETS FATED TO ETERNAL ENMITY WITH ONE ANOTHER.

AND UNTO THE HELL THAT WAS APOKOLIPS CAME *DARKSEID*, MALICE PERSONIFIED, A MERCILESS TYRANT WHO DEMANDED UNWAVERING DEVOTION AND ABJECT FEAR FROM ALL HIS SUBJECTS.

THE LOWLY FOOL ENOUGH TO DEFY DARKSEID FACED THE *OMEGA EFFECT*, A POWER ABLE TO SEEK OUT AND PUNISH ANY TREACHERY LITERALLY *BEHIND* DARKSEID'S BACK.

AS TOTAL WAR THREATENED TO ANNIHILATE THE TWIN WORLDS AS IT HAD THEIR PRECURSOR, DARKSEID FORGED A FRAGILE PACT WITH HIGHFATHER OF NEW GENESIS.

TO ENSURE A TENTATIVE PEACE, THEY TRADED SONS, DARKSEID GIVING UP HIS OWN SCION *ORION* TO BE REARED AS HIGHFATHER'S OWN WHILE A PRINCE OF NEW GENESIS WAS CONSIGNED TO AN APOKOLIPTIAN ORPHANAGE.

LIVE FOR DARKSEID
DIE FOR
DARKSEID IS
DARKSEID

LITTLE DID DARKSEID REALIZE--OR *CARE*--THAT HIS FIRSTBORN WOULD ONE DAY CHANNEL HIS BARELY SUPPRESSED BERSERKER SIDE TO COMBAT HIS FATHER'S INCALCULABLE EVIL.

OF COURSE, *OTHER* SONS WOULD JOSTLE FOR DARKSEID'S FAVOR--KALIBAK THE CRUEL AND GRAYVEN THE CONQUEROR ARE BUT TWO OF HIS BASTARD SPAWN SCATTERED ACROSS THE COSMOS.

WHEN RENEWED CONFLICT AGAINST NEW GENESIS STALEMATED AT EVERY TURN, DARKSEID TURNED HIS ATTENTION TOWARD ANOTHER WORLD.

BUT EARTH'S HEROES--PERHAPS *NEWER* GODS IN THEIR OWN RIGHT--ALWAYS DENIED DARKSEID HIS PRIZE.

ON DISTANT EARTH, DARKSEID BELIEVED HE MIGHT CLAIM THE SO-CALLED *ANTI-LIFE EQUATION*, THE MEANS TO USURP ALL FREE WILL AND THUS CONTROL EVERY SENTIENT BEING IN THE UNIVERSE.

SUBSEQUENTLY, THE DREAD LORD OF APOKOLIPS WAGED WAR UPON THE SMALL PLANET, TURNING PUBLIC OPINION AGAINST ITS COSTUMED LEGENDS, DECIMATING ITS ONCE-IMMORTAL AMAZONS, AND PLOTTING TO CORRUPT INNOCENT SOULS IN HIS MANY SINISTER STRATAGEMS TO GAIN A FOOTHOLD ON EARTH.

EARTH'S CHAMPIONS BECAME MERE PAWNS IN DARKSEID'S DIABOLICAL GAME TO GOVERN NOT JUST THE KNOWN UNIVERSE, BUT THE ENTIRETY OF EXISTENCE ACROSS TIME AND SPACE!

BUT ULTIMATELY, THE STORY OF DARKSEID IS ABOUT A TYRANT'S REACH EXCEEDING HIS GRASP. AND SO, INEVITABLY, THERE COMES A TIME...

...WHEN EVEN DARKSEID MUST DIE.

POWERS AND WEAPONS:

A being of unparalleled strength, Darkseid nevertheless preferred not to sully his gloves with hand-to-hand combat unless provoked to action. His eyes emitted the formidable Omega Effect, ray beams that could disintegrate, teleport, or resurrect depending on the dread lord's wishes.

ESSENTIAL STORYLINES:

- *Jack Kirby's Fourth World Omnibus Vol. 1-4*
- *Legion of Super-Heroes: The Great Darkness Saga*
- *Legends*
- *Cosmic Odyssey*
- *Countdown Vol. 1-4*

THE ORIGIN OF DEADSHOT

Writer
SCOTT BEATTY
Artist
FREDDIE E. WILLIAMS II
Colorist
HI-FI
Letterer
KEN LOPEZ
Editor
ELISABETH V. GEHRLEIN

IF THERE'S A BULLET WITH YOUR NAME ON IT, PRAY THAT DEADSHOT DOESN'T HAVE IT.

THOUGH BORN OF AFFLUENCE, *FLOYD LAWTON* MASQUERADED AS THE SHARPSHOOTING "HERO" *DEADSHOT*--*DISARMING* RATHER THAN *KILLING* HIS OPPONENTS--AS A RUSE TO TAKE OVER GOTHAM CITY'S CRIME RACKETS.

LAWTON MIGHT HAVE SUCCEEDED IF GOTHAM'S *OTHER* SELF-APPOINTED GUARDIAN HAD NOT ALTERED DEADSHOT'S GUNSIGHTS, MAKING HIS AIM--LIKE HIS INTENTIONS--*LESS* THAN TRUE.

BATTLING BATMAN ONCE IS *HUBRIS*. TARGETING HIM TWICE OR MORE IS INARGUABLY A *DEATHWISH*, WHICH EXPLAINS SO MANY OF DEADSHOT'S DECISIONS OVER THE YEARS.

WHY ELSE WOULD DEADSHOT AGREE TO COMMUTE A LENGTHY PRISON SENTENCE TO TIME-SERVED IN EXCHANGE FOR SERVICE IN THE SO-CALLED *"SUICIDE SQUAD,"* A TEAM OF *EXPENDABLE* GOVERNMENT OPERATIVES?

SURVIVING THE SQUAD DESPITE HIS OTHERWISE SELF-DESTRUCTIVE TRAJECTORY, DEADSHOT CONSIDERED HOLSTERING HIS GUNS FOREVER AND SETTLING DOWN IN STAR CITY.

BUT WITH HIS NEW FAMILY IN THE CROSSHAIRS OF VENGEFUL VILLAINS, DEADSHOT REALIZED THAT THE PAST, LIKE THE TRACE OF GUNPOWDER, IS HARD TO WIPE AWAY COMPLETELY.

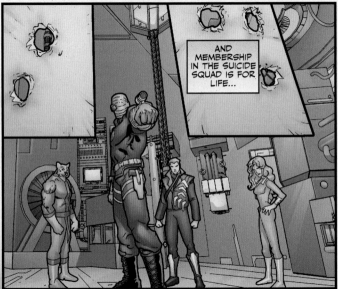

AND MEMBERSHIP IN THE SUICIDE SQUAD IS FOR LIFE...

...OR DEATH.

WANTED

WANTED

Y RATHAWAY

JAMES JESSE

POWERS AND WEAPONS:

Gifted with unerring aim, Deadshot is likely the world's best—and deadliest—marksman, proficient with nearly every model and caliber of firearm. Deadshot prefers high-powered wrist-blaster gauntlets, as well as modified Glock 9 mm pistols able to fire grenades and other specialized projectiles.

ESSENTIAL STORYLINES:

- BATMAN: STRANGE APPARITIONS
- SHOWCASE PRESENTS: SUICIDE SQUAD 1
- DEADSHOT 1-5

THE *ORIGIN* OF DEATHSTROKE THE TERMINATOR

SCOTT BEATTY
Writer

TONY DANIEL
Penciler

JON GLAPION
Inker

HI-FI
Colorist

KEN LOPEZ
Letterer

ELISABETH V. GEHRLEIN
Editor

DEATHSTROKE THE TERMINATOR created by **MARV WOLFMAN** and **GEORGE PÉREZ**

THE ARMY MADE *MAJOR SLADE WILSON* ALL HE COULD BE...

...AND THEN IT MADE HIM *BETTER.*

VIA EXPERIMENTAL HORMONE THERAPY, HE BECAME A *SUPER-TROOPER.*

UNBEKNOWNST TO SLADE'S SUPERIORS, THE PROCEDURE BOOSTED HIS BRAIN CAPACITY, INCREASING HIS COORDINATION AND STAMINA TO SUPERHUMAN LEVELS.

RETIRING FROM MILITARY SERVICE, SLADE USED HIS NEWLY ACQUIRED ABILITIES AS AN ASSASSIN-FOR-HIRE.

UNFORTUNATELY, YOUNG JOSEPH WILSON WAS TARGETED AS A RESULT OF HIS FATHER'S MERCENARY CAREER AS *DEATHSTROKE THE TERMINATOR.*

FOR HER SON'S SLASHED THROAT, *ADELINE WILSON* TOOK HER HUSBAND'S RIGHT EYE.

FORTUNATELY, SLADE'S ENHANCED REFLEXES SAVED HIS LIFE; THE SHARP-SHOOTING ADELINE HAD INTENDED TO *KILL* HIM.

WHEN DEATHSTROKE REFUSED A H.I.V.E. CONTRACT TO KILL THE TEEN TITANS...

...HE SEALED ANOTHER SON'S FATE.

TRAGICALLY, GRANT WILSON'S *RAVAGER* FAILED TO LIVE UP TO HIS FATHER'S INSIDIOUS IMAGE.

BLAMING THE TITANS FOR GRANT'S DEATH, DEATHSTROKE AGREED TO COMPLETE THE CONTRACT IN HIS OWN WAY.

THE TURNCOAT *TERRA* WOULD BE SLADE'S JUDAS GOAT, INFILTRATING THE TITANS, EARNING THEIR TRUST, AND THEN LEADING THEM STRAIGHT TO THE H.I.V.E. FOR SLAUGHTER.

...T THE TRAP COLLAPSED WHEN JOSEPH WILSON, TAKING THE NAME JERICHO, JOINED THE TITANS' ...HT FOR THEIR LIVES AGAINST AN UNSTABLE TERRA.

IRONICALLY, SLADE LATER SAVED THE TITANS FROM AN AZARATHIAN-POSSESSED JOSEPH.

TO SPARE HIS SON'S SOUL, DEATHSTROKE TERMINATED JERICHO *HIMSELF.*

LATER, SLADE ATTEMPTED TO TAKE HIS ILLEGITIMATE DAUGHTER, *ROSE WILSON,* AS HIS APPRENTICE. SHE WAS SKILLED WITH WEAPONS...

...AND LOYAL TO A *FAULT.*

BUT ALONGSIDE A RESURRECTED JERICHO, ROSE'S RAVAGER JOINED THE TITANS--

--PROMPTING SLADE TO ASSEMBLE A VILLAINOUS *TITANS EAST.*

IN THIS WAY, SLADE FORCED THE TEEN HEROES TO GIVE HIS CHILDREN SOMETHING THAT HE, IN THE END, NEVER COULD...

...A FAMILY.

Powers & Weapons:

ABLE TO USE 90% OF HIS BRAIN CAPACITY, DEATHSTROKE THUS POSSESSES HEIGHTENED SENSES, REFLEXES, AND PHYSICAL ACUMEN. HIS ARSENAL IS EXTENSIVE AND, WITH HIS AUGMENTED PHYSIQUE, HE CAN TURN ANY OBJECT INTO A DEADLY WEAPON. NEVERTHELESS, HE PREFERS HIS BROADSWORD, BLASTING BO STAFF, AND AUTOMATIC PISTOLS.

Essential Storylines:

- THE NEW TEEN TITANS 2
- THE NEW TEEN TITANS: THE JUDAS CONTRACT
- TEEN TITANS: A KID'S GAME
- TEEN TITANS: TITANS EAST

THE ORIGIN OF DESAAD

SYCOPHANT.

BOOTLICKER.

SADIST OF THE HIGHEST ORDER.

DESAAD.

TO SERVE AT THE LEFT HAND OF DARKSEID, ONE MUST MAKE CERTAIN SACRIFICES.

GREAKKHHHH

AN EQUAL-OPPORTUNITY HENCHMAN, THE VENGEFUL DESAAD ONCE FORGED AN ILL-FATED ALLIANCE WITH DARKSEID'S OWN MOTHER... QUEEN HEGGRA.

DESAAD MURDERED DARKSEID'S LOVER, THE SORCERESS SULI, TO PAVE THE WAY FOR DARK-SEID'S ARRANGED MARRIAGE TO THE CONCUBINE TIGGRA, AS PER THE QUEEN-MOTHER'S WICKED WISHES.

DARKSEID WAS NEITHER FOOLED...

...NOR AMUSED.

WRITER:
SCOTT BEATTY
ARTIST:
WALTER SIMONSON
LETTERER:
JOHN WORKMAN
COLORIST:
HI-FI
EDITOR:
ELISABETH V. GEHRLEIN

SIMONSON 9-24-07

DESAAD CREATED BY JACK KIRBY.

TO SPARE HIS OWN MISERABLE LIFE, DESAAD WAS OFFERED THE RARE OPPORTUNITY TO REGAIN DARKSEID'S CONFIDENCE...

...WITH **ANOTHER** SACRIFICE.

THUS REDEEMED, DESAAD ROSE THROUGH THE COURT OF APOKOLIPS AS DARKSEID'S MASTER INQUISITOR...

...HIS EVERY PLEASURE ELICITED THROUGH PAIN.

AND THE OCCASIONAL **TREACHERY**—INVARIABLY MET WITH DARKSEID'S OWN UNIQUE AND QUITE FINAL PUNISHMENT.

HOW FORTUNATE FOR DESAAD THAT EVEN THE MOST **OPPORTUNISTIC** SERVANTS HAVE A PLACE IN THE COURT OF DARKSEID...AND SOME EVEN WARM A TINY SPOT IN HIS BLACKENED HEART.

Powers & Weapons:

DESAAD LACKS ANY REAL POWERS, EXCEPT FOR HIS GENIUS IN DEVISING INSTRUMENTS OF TORTURE AND WEAPONS OF MASS DESTRUCTION, NOT TO MENTION HIS UNENDING SCHEMES TO CLAIM THE THRONE OF APOKOLIPS FOR HIMSELF.

Essential Storylines:

- JACK KIRBY'S FOURTH WORLD OMNIBUS VOL. 1-4
- ECLIPSO 10

Best Death:

- ORION 11

THE ORIGIN OF DOOMSDAY

WRITER-SCOTT BEATTY
ARTIST-JON BOGDANOVE
LETTERER-**KEN LOPEZ** COLORIST-**HI-FI**
EDITOR-**ELISABETH V. GEHRLEIN**
DOOMSDAY CREATED BY BREEDING, ORDWAY,
L. SIMONSON, STERN, AND JURGENS

MONSTERS AREN'T BORN, THEY'RE *MADE*.

MILLENNNIA AGO ON AN INHOSPITABLE KRYPTON, THE SCIENTIST *BERTRON* SOUGHT TO MAKE THE ULTIMATE LIFE-FORM. UNSUCCESSFUL AT FIRST, BERTRON TRIED AGAIN...

AND AGAIN AND AGAIN, SALVAGING CELLS FROM EACH FAILED EXPERIMENT UNTIL THE PERFECT BEAST WAS BUILT, AN UNKILLABLE MONSTER GENETICALLY IMPRINTED TO *SURVIVE*.

ALSO IMPRINTED WAS THE MEMORY OF THE INNUMERABLE DEATHS DOOMSDAY SUFFERED TO BECOME HIS "FATHER'S" SUPERIOR BEING.

BERTRON WOULD KNOW THAT IN THE NANO-MOMENTS BEFORE HIS OWN VERY SAVAGE DEMISE.

TO SPARE PEACEFUL CATALON THE PLANET'S SUPERPOWERFUL ROYAL FAMILY SACRIFICED THEIR OWN LIFE FORCES TO CREATE *THE RADIANT*, A BEING OF PURE ENERGY WHO STOPPED THE UNSTOPPABLE.

IN THE AFTERMATH, DOOMSDAY CLUNG TO A DEPARTING SUPPLY SHIP AND RAGED ACROSS THE STARS.

UNFORTUNATELY, THE CATALONIANS GAVE DOOMSDAY THEIR CUSTOMARY FUNERAL RITES, BINDING THE MONSTER'S BODY SO THAT HIS SPIRIT WOULD NOT RAGE IN THE AFTERLIFE.

PROPELLED INTO THE VOID OF SPACE, DOOMSDAY'S ASTRAL HEARSE WOULD HAVE DRIFTED ETERNALLY IF NOT FOR ERRANT ASTEROIDS THAT BROUGHT HIS IMMORTAL BODY CRASHING DOWN UPON AN UNSUSPECTING *EARTH.*

THERE, *TWO* SONS OF KRYPTON FROM DIFFERANT ERAS MET IN FATAL CONFLICT, THEIR DEATHBLOWS SHAKING THE PLANET TO ITS CORE.

THANKFULLY, *SUPERMAN* WOULD RETURN FROM DEATH...

AS WOULD DOOMSDAY...

AGAIN...

AND AGAIN...

ESSENTIAL STORYLINES:

· THE DEATH OF SUPERMAN
· SUPERMAN/DOOMSDAY: HUNTER/PREY
· SUPERMAN: OUR WORLDS AT WAR
· SUPERMAN: IN THE NAME OF GOG
· INFINITE CRISIS

POWERS AND WEAPONS:

Invulnerable. Indefatigable. Immortal. Doomsday does not need to eat or breathe, instead drawing and storing energy to fuel his superstrong body from solar radiation. His body has no internal organs and is nearly entirely solid, making him impervious to almost any attack. Designed to evolve with each "death," Doomsday becomes more powerful with each resurrection and cannot be killed the same way twice.

THE ORIGIN OF DR. LIGHT

WRITER--SCOTT BEATTY
ARTIST--HOWARD PORTER
LETTERER--TRAVIS LANHAM
EDITOR--ELISABETH V. GEHRLEIN

THE TERM *EPIPHANY* LITERALLY MEANS "TO SEE THE LIGHT," TO EXPERIENCE A MOMENT OF PROFOUND REALIZATION AS IF ILLUMINATED FROM ABOVE.

PHYSICIST ARTHUR LIGHT'S EPIPHANY WAS REALIZING THAT HE DESIRED WEALTH AND POWER MORE THAN ANY NOBEL PRIZE OR SCIENTIFIC ACCOLADE.

AND SO HE SET OUT TO EDUCATE THE *LESS* ENLIGHTENED WITH HIS OWN INVENTIVE LIGHT WEAPONS, PATENTS PENDING.

HOWEVER, CHALLENGING THE JUSTICE LEAGUE OF AMERICA IN HIS FIRST EVIL ENTERPRISE WOULD PROVE TO BE THE *FIRST* IN A LONG HISTORY OF BAD IDEAS FROM THE MIND OF DR. LIGHT.

RETURNING TO THE LEAGUE'S LIMELIGHT WOULD BE HIS *SECOND.*

A COWARD BY NATURE, DR. LIGHT SURREPTITIOUSLY BEAMED INTO THE JLA'S SATELLITE HEADQUARTERS TO CATCH HIS FOES UNAWARE. WHEN HE FOUND THE HEROES AWAY ON A MISSION OF MERCY, DR. LIGHT INSTEAD OPTED TO INFLICT *COLLATERAL DAMAGE.*

ASSAULTING SUE DIBNY, THE ELONGATED MAN'S WIFE, WASN'T DR. LIGHT'S BRIGHTEST IDEA, DESPITE THE *SATISFACTION* IT GAVE HIM.

MEMBERS OPTED TO SILENCE DR. LIGHT BY STRIPPING HIM OF THE MEMORY OF HIS VILE ACT.

BUT THE SORCERESS ZATANNA'S MAGICAL *MINDWIPE* PARTIALLY (AND UNINTENTIONALLY) LOBOTOMIZED LIGHT.

MADE *LESS THAN BRILLIANT* AS A RESULT, AN INCREASINGLY INCOMPETENT DR. LIGHT FORMED THE SO-CALLED *FEARSOME FIVE* TO RECAPTURE HIS FORMER VILLAINOUS GLORY.

OF COURSE, HE WAS *LESS THAN SUCCESSFUL*, AND AGAIN AND AGAIN THE TEEN TITANS REVEALED WHAT A BUFFOON HE HAD BECOME.

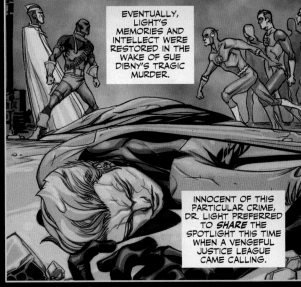

EVENTUALLY, LIGHT'S MEMORIES AND INTELLECT WERE RESTORED IN THE WAKE OF SUE DIBNY'S TRAGIC MURDER.

INNOCENT OF THIS PARTICULAR CRIME, DR. LIGHT PREFERRED TO *SHARE* THE SPOTLIGHT THIS TIME WHEN A VENGEFUL JUSTICE LEAGUE CAME CALLING.

NOW, BRIMMING WITH *NEW* BRIGHT IDEAS, BADDER THAN BEFORE IN MANY WAYS, DR. LIGHT WISHES ONLY TO SHARE HIS FLASHES OF GENIUS WITH THE "HEROES" WHO HUMBLED HIM...

...AS WELL AS THEIR LOVED ONES.

POWERS AND WEAPONS:

DR. LIGHT'S STUDY OF ILLUMINATION HAS YIELDED VARIOUS ADVANCED LIGHT-BASED WEAPONS, INCLUDING SOLID LIGHT PROJECTORS, PHOTON BLASTERS, SPATIAL WARP GENERATORS, AND ILLUSION CASTERS, TO LIST BUT A FEW. THOUGH ORIGINALLY WIELDING THESE WEAPONS IN THE FORM OF RAY GUNS AND OTHER HAND-HELD APPARATUS, DR. LIGHT INCORPORATED MUCH OF HIS ORIGINAL AND STOLEN TECHNOLOGY INTO MICROCIRCUITRY WOVEN THROUGHOUT HIS COSTUME. HE AVOIDS HAND-TO-HAND COMBAT WHENEVER POSSIBLE.

ESSENTIAL STORYLINES:

· JUSTICE LEAGUE OF AMERICA 12
· THE NEW TEEN TITANS 3, 7
· IDENTITY CRISIS
· SALVATION RUN

AFFILIATIONS:

· THE FEARSOME FIVE
· SUICIDE SQUAD
· SECRET SOCIETY OF SUPER-VILLAINS
· INJUSTICE LEAGUE

GOOD AND EVIL, DAY AND NIGHT, TO EVERYTHING THERE IS AN EQUAL BUT OPPOSITE FORCE...

THE ORIGIN OF ECLIPSO

Writer -- SCOTT BEATTY
Artist -- PHIL WINSLADE
Letterer -- TRAVIS LANHAM
Colorist -- HI-FI
Editor -- ELISABETH V. GEHRLEIN

IN THE BEGINNING, GOD'S *SPIRIT OF WRATH* WAS MADE FLESH TO PUNISH THE WICKED AND WASH THE EARTH CLEAN OF VICE AND INIQUITY.

WRATH, BY DEFINITION, IS DRIVEN LARGELY BY ANGER. WHEREAS *VENGEANCE* REQUIRES A LIGHTER TOUCH...

AS THE OLD TESTAMENT GAVE WAY TO THE FAIRER AND MORE BALANCED GOD OF THE NEW, THE SPIRIT OF WRATH WAS STRIPPED OF RANK AND PRIVILEGES BY ITS SUCCESSOR, *THE SPECTRE.*

SPLIT ASUNDER BY GOD'S NEWLY ANOINTED *SPIRIT OF VENGEANCE,* WRATH'S PHYSICALITY WAS TRAPPED WITHIN THE *HEART OF DARKNESS,* A BLACK DIAMOND MINED ON DISTANT APOKOLIPS THAT BROUGHT ONLY WOE AND MISERY TO ANYONE WHO CAME INTO ITS POSSESSION.

WHAT REMAINED OF GOD'S WRATH WAS BANISHED QUITE APPROPRIATELY TO THE *DARK SIDE* OF THE MOON.

BUT NOT FOR LONG...

A SINGLE, WELL-PLACED STRIKE CAN SPLIT A SEEMINGLY INDESTRUCTIBLE DIAMOND. THE HEART OF DARKNESS WAS THUS *SHATTERED,* A THOUSAND SHARDS OF EQUAL CUT AND CARAT, EACH CONTAINING A SLIVER OF EVIL, WERE SCATTERED ACROSS THE GLOBE...

DR. BRUCE GORDON DISCOVERED HIS IN A SOUTH PACIFIC JUNGLE.

WHILE ATTEMPTING TO FILM A RARE SOLAR ECLIPSE, GORDON WAS SCRATCHED BY ONE SUCH CURSED GEMSTONE BY THE MADDENED TRIBAL SEER *MOPHIR.*

AND SO BEGAN GORDON'S LONG STRANGE TRIP IN THE COMPAN OF HIS EVIL ALTE

THE SOLAR SCIENTIST'S SELF-APPOINTED CRUSADE BECAME THWARTING HIS *DARK HALF* AT EVERY TURN.

IN TIME, THE TWO WERE FINALLY SEPARATED--*YIN* FROM *YANG*--AS ECLIPSO SOUGHT TO PLUNGE EARTH INTO ETERNAL DARKNESS AND DESPAIR BY POSSESSING THE PLANET'S STALWART SUPERHEROES.

FOR SOME, RESISTANCE WAS FATALLY *FUTILE.*

TO AVENGE HIS SLAIN SISTER, *ALEX MONTEZ* ETCHED HIS SKIN IN MYSTIC RUNES AND INJECTED HIMSELF WITH LIQUEFIED BLACK DIAMONDS, THUS IMPRISONING ECLIPSO WITHIN HIS OWN BODY.

BUT, FEARING ECLIPSO'S BOASTS THAT HE WOULD ESCAPE EVENTUALLY, MONTEZ CHOSE SUICIDE IN A MISGUIDED ATTEMPT TO CAGE THE EVIL WITHIN HIM FOR ALL TIME.

OF COURSE, ECLIPSO SOUGHT A NEW AND MORE *SUGGESTIBLE* HOST. DIAMONDS, EVEN BLACK-HEARTED BAUBLES, ARE A GIRL'S BEST FRIEND AFTER ALL...

IN *JEAN LORING,* ECLIPSO FOUND A WILLING SOUL MATE, BOTH DESIRING REVENGE UPON EARTH'S BRIGHTLY HUED HEROES.

THE SPIRIT OF WRATH FORGED AN UNLIKELY ALLIANCE WITH THE SPECTRE, SEDUCING THE SPIRIT OF VENGEANCE AND WAGING GENOCIDAL WAR ON EARTH'S MYSTICS AND MAGES, A CONFLICT THAT LED TO A CLIMACTIC CONFRONTATION WITH CAPTAIN MARVEL AND THE NEWLY FORMED *SHADOWPACT.*

IN DEFEAT, SHE WAS TRAPPED BY PERPETUAL DAYLIGHT IN A PERMANENT ORBIT AROUND THE SUN, STILL CASTING A LONG SHADOW ACROSS EARTH. AGAIN, ECLIPSO'S ESCAPE WAS *INEVITABLE.*

EVEN NOW, ECLIPSO DARKENS EVERYTHING SHE TOUCHES.

CONSIDER IT CORRUPTION OF THE COSTUMED INCORRUPTIBLE, OR, MORE APTLY...

SEDUCTION OF THE INNOCENT.

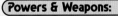

Powers & Weapons:

A MAGICAL BEING OF INCALCULABLE STRENGTH, ECLIPSO HAS DEMONSTRATED THE POWER OF FLIGHT AND THE ABILITY TO EMIT DEADLY RAYS OF DARK LIGHT FROM HIS/HER LEFT EYE AND FOCUSED THROUGH ECLIPSO'S BLACK DIAMOND. ECLIPSO IS ABLE TO POSSESS ANYONE WHO TOUCHES THE CURSED GEM, CONTROLLING THE HOST'S POWERS TO ECLIPSO'S OWN TWISTED ENDS.

Essential Storylines:

- HOUSE OF SECRETS 61
- ECLIPSO: THE DARKNESS WITHIN 1-2
- ECLIPSO 1-18
- DAY OF VENGEANCE
- COUNTDOWN

THE ORIGIN OF ELONGATED Man

MARK WAID
Writer

KEVIN NOWLAN
Art & Colors

NICK J. NAP
Letters

STEPHEN WACKER & HARVEY RICHARDS
Editors

GROWING UP IN THE TINY BURG OF WAYMORE, NEBRASKA, GAWKY RALPH DIBNY--A BORN DETECTIVE--NEVER STOPPED LOOKING FOR THAT WHICH HE FOUND EVERY DAY:

ATTENTION.

RALPH WAS FASCINATED BY CONTORTIONISTS--PERFORMERS WHO WON APPLAUSE BY DOING SOMETHING FOR WHICH LANKY RALPH ALREADY HAD A KNACK.

EVERY "RUBBER MAN" THAT RALPH TALKED TO AND EMULATED HAD ONE THING IN COMMON:

A TASTE FOR A SOFT DRINK CALLED "GINGOLD."

SUSPECTING SOME SORT OF "TRADE SECRET," RALPH DISTILLED THE ESSENCE OF THE RARE GINGO FRUIT USED IN GINGOLD AND ACQUIRED A TASTE FOR IT--

--UNAWARE THAT, IN ITS CONCENTRATED FORM, IT COULD BE LETHAL.

LUCK SAVED RALPH DIBNY FROM TOXIC ALLERGIC REACTION. INSTEAD, THE MODIFIED GINGOLD TRIGGERED SOMETHING IN RALPH'S BIOCHEMISTRY--

--ALLOWING HIM TO STRETCH HIS BODY LIKE ELASTIC.

CALLING HIMSELF "THE ELONGATED MAN," RALPH BEGAN A CAREER AS A COSTUMED SLEUTH AND TRAVELED THE WORLD WITH HIS WEALTHY BRIDE, SUE DEARBON.

DAILY NEWS
OCEANOGRAPHER FOUND MURDERED IN ONE MAN BATHYSPHERE

CLAD IN AN ARRAY OF COLORFUL UNIFORMS, RALPH BECAME THE FIRST SUPER-HERO TO MAKE HIS SECRET IDENTITY PUBLIC AND BECAME FAMOUS AS A MEMBER OF THE JUSTICE LEAGUE OF AMERICA.

AFTER SUE WAS MURDERED, HOWEVER, RALPH'S CHARMED LIFE LOST ITS GLAMOUR. HAVING SINCE ABANDONED GINGOLD, HE REMAINS A DETECTIVE--

SUE DIBNY

--INVESTIGATING THE GREATEST MYSTERY THERE IS.

WHERE ARE YOU, SUE?

POWERS AND WEAPONS:

When dosed with Gingold, detective Ralph Dibny's body becomes super-elastic. Ralph specializes in a gift for lateral thinking that even The Batman cannot match.

ESSENTIAL STORYLINES:

- Showcase Presents: The Elongated Man
- Identity Crisis

The Origin of FELIX FAUST

WRITER--SCOTT BEATTY
ARTIST--JESUS SAIZ
COLORIST--HI-FI
LETTERER--TRAVIS LANHAM
EDITOR--ELISABETH V. GEHRLEIN

IN THE REALM OF MYSTICISM, A *SOUL* CAN BE THE MOST VALUABLE CURRENCY OF ALL.

SEVEN MILLENNIA AGO, SORCERER FELIX FAUST CHALLENGED THE WIZARD-KING NOMMO, RULER OF MAGNIFICENT KOR, FOR POSSESSION OF THE BURNING ENIGMA CALLED THE *FLAME OF LIFE.*

HAVING LITTLE TO TRADE EXCEPT HIS OWN MALEFIC MAGICKS, THE GREEDY FAUST WAS BANISHED FROM THE BARGAINING TABLE AS KOR CRUMBLED TO HISTORY.

FELIX DID NOT ESCAPE HIS OTHERDIMENSIONAL PRISON UNTIL THE EARLY TWENTIETH CENTURY...

...WHEN OCCULT DABBLER *DEKAN DRACHE* MADE HIS OWN ONE-SIDED FAUSTIAN PACT.

THUS DID FELIX FAUST EMBARK ON MANY GLOBE-SPANNING JOURNEYS TO REGAIN MAGICAL POWER THROUGH TALISMANS LONG FORGOTTEN EXCEPT BY *HIM.*

ALL THE BETTER TO SUMMON FORTH DEMONS, *THREE* TO BE EXACT--

--*RATH, GHAST,* AND *ABNEGAZAR*--

--AND STRIKE A BARGAIN OF HIS OWN, RELEASING THEM FROM DAMNATION IN EXCHANGE FOR MYSTICAL OMNIPOTENCE.

TO CAST THE SPELL THAT WOULD FREE THE *DEMONS THREE*, FAUST COMPELLED THE JUSTICE LEAGUE OF AMERICA TO FIND THREE OBJECTS OF POWER:

THE SILVER WHEEL OF NYORLATH, THE GREEN BELL OF UTHOOL, AND *THE RED JAR OF CALYTHOS.*

THOUGH THEY WERE PARALYZED IN *BODY,* FAUST DID NOT BIND THE HEROES' *MINDS...*

...PERMITTING AQUAMAN TO TELEPATHICALLY SUMMON A SCHOOL OF FLYING FISH...

...WHICH BROKE FAUST'S CONCENTRATION AND DEFEATED THE WILY WIZARD.

AND SO IT WENT, FAUST CALLING CREATURES FROM BEYOND...

...AND THE JUSTICE LEAGUE PUTTING THEM BACK IN THEIR PRIVATE HELLS.

MORE RECENTLY, FAUST MASQUERADED AS THE SORCERER *NABU* TO TEMPT *RALPH DIBNY,* THE ELONGATED MAN, WITH THE MYSTIC MEANS TO RESURRECT HIS MURDERED WIFE SUE.

BUT RALPH'S TWITCHING NOSE SMELLED A MYSTERY...

...AND THE DUCTILE DETECTIVE TURNED THE TABLES ON FAUST...

...TRAPPING HIM AND THE SUPREME TEMPTER *NERON* WITHIN THE TOWER SANCTUM OF DR. FATE.

NOT ONE TO MAKE THE SAME MAGICAL MISTAKE TWICE, FAUST TEMPTED *BLACK ADAM* WITH THE PROMISE TO RAISE HIS BELOVED *ISIS* FROM DEATH'S EMBRACE.

THIS TIME, HOWEVER, HE OPTED FOR A SIMPLER RUSE, SWITCHING THE SKELETON OF ISIS WITH THE BONES OF RALPH DIBNY AND THUS CONFOUNDING THE RESURRECTION SPELL.

A TRUE FAUSTIAN PACT INVOLVES DEFERRED PAYMENT.

AND THE PRICE FELIX WILL PAY FOR DECEIVING THE NOTORIOUSLY VENGEFUL BLACK ADAM REMAINS TO BE SEEN.

POWERS AND WEAPONS:

In his millennia on Earth, Faust has studied the occult to amass formidable talents in spellcasting and the summoning of demons. What Faust lacks in true magical power he makes up for in his willingness to sell his soul or sacrifice others--including his own children--to obtain mystical might.

ESSENTIAL STORYLINES:

- Justice League of America 10
- Secret Origins 27
- 52
- Black Adam: The Dark Age

AFFILIATIONS:

- The Crime Champions
- Secret Society of Super-Villains
- Injustice League of America

THE ORIGIN OF
FIRESTORM
THE NUCLEAR MAN

MARK WAID — WRITER
JAMAL IGLE — PENCILLER
INKER-KEITH CHAMPAGNE
COLORIST-ALEX SINCLAIR
LETTERER-TRAVIS LANHAM
ASST. EDITOR-HARVEY RICHARDS
ASSOC. EDITOR-JEANINE SCHAEFER
EDITOR-MICHAEL SIGLAIN
FIRESTORM CREATED BY
GERRY CONWAY AND AL MILGROM

TOO BROKE TO LEAVE HOME, TOO TIMID TO STAND UP TO AN ABUSIVE FATHER...

...IF TEENAGER *JASON RUSCH* WAS EVER GOING TO STOP BEING A PUNCHING BAG, HE WAS GOING TO HAVE TO LEARN TO MAKE SOME *CHANGES.*

DESPERATE FOR COLLEGE TUITION, JASON ACCEPTED A ONE-TIME COURIER JOB WITH A KNOWN CRIMINAL. THE DELIVERY TOOK JASON INTO THE DESOLATE OUTSKIRTS OF DETROIT--

--AND, BY CHANCE, HEADLONG INTO AN *ATOMIC BLAST.*

A HERO NAMED *FIRESTORM* HAD BEEN FATALLY WOUNDED. FALLING DIRECTLY IN JASON'S PATH, FIRESTORM'S NUCLEAR LIFEFORCE CASCADED INTO THE BOY'S BODY--

--FUSING JASON TO THE *FIRESTORM MATRIX*, AN INTERDIMENSIONAL ENERGY THAT GIVES ITS HOST THE POWER OF *ATOMIC TRANSMUTATION*.

BY MELDING WITH OTHERS, TEMPORARILY MERGING THEIR BODIES AND MINDS WITH HIS OWN, JASON COULD BECOME A *SUPER-HERO*.

THOUGH THIS CARRIED WITH IT NEW RESPONSIBILITIES, IT WAS EXACTLY THE PUSH JASON NEEDED TO REARRANGE HIS WORLD.

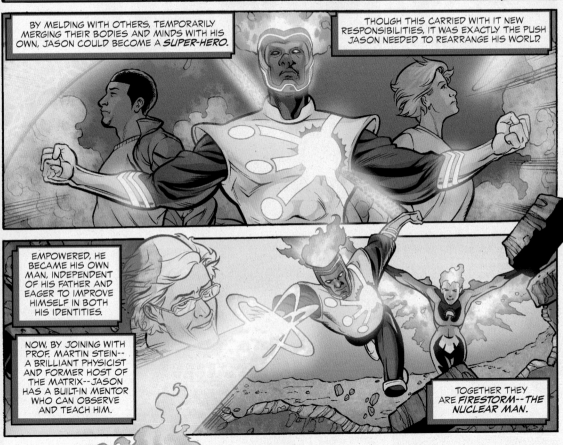

EMPOWERED, HE BECAME HIS OWN MAN, INDEPENDENT OF HIS FATHER AND EAGER TO IMPROVE HIMSELF IN BOTH HIS IDENTITIES.

NOW, BY JOINING WITH PROF. MARTIN STEIN-- A BRILLIANT PHYSICIST AND FORMER HOST OF THE MATRIX--JASON HAS A BUILT-IN MENTOR WHO CAN OBSERVE AND TEACH HIM.

TOGETHER THEY ARE *FIRESTORM--THE NUCLEAR MAN.*

POWERS AND WEAPONS:

Firestorm's energies allow him to atomically transmute inorganic matter and throw concussive "fusion blasts." They also give him superhuman strength, durability and flying powers, and allow him to absorb radiation harmlessly.

ESSENTIAL STORYLINES:

- Firestorm 1-4 (2004)
- Firestorm 20-22 (2006)
- Firestorm: Reborn TPB
- Identity Crisis
- Infinite Crisis

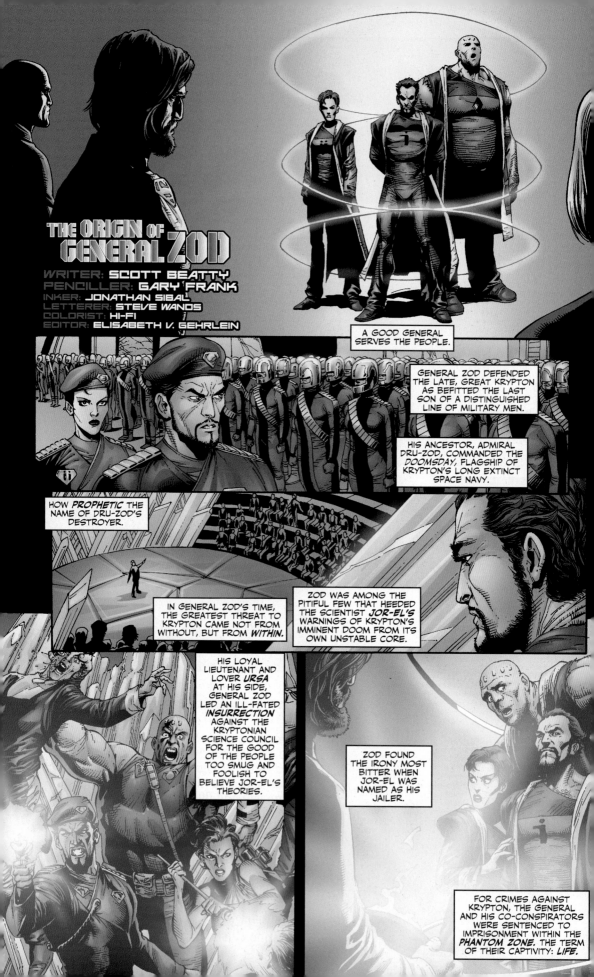

THE ORIGIN OF GENERAL ZOD

WRITER: SCOTT BEATTY
PENCILLER: GARY FRANK
INKER: JONATHAN SIBAL
LETTERER: STEVE WANDS
COLORIST: HI-FI
EDITOR: ELISABETH V. GEHRLEIN

A GOOD GENERAL SERVES THE PEOPLE.

GENERAL ZOD DEFENDED THE LATE, GREAT KRYPTON AS BEFITTED THE LAST SON OF A DISTINGUISHED LINE OF MILITARY MEN.

HIS ANCESTOR, ADMIRAL DRU-ZOD, COMMANDED THE *DOOMSDAY,* FLAGSHIP OF KRYPTON'S LONG EXTINCT SPACE NAVY.

HOW *PROPHETIC* THE NAME OF DRU-ZOD'S DESTROYER.

IN GENERAL ZOD'S TIME, THE GREATEST THREAT TO KRYPTON CAME NOT FROM WITHOUT, BUT FROM *WITHIN.*

ZOD WAS AMONG THE PITIFUL FEW THAT HEEDED THE SCIENTIST *JOR-EL'S* WARNINGS OF KRYPTON'S IMMINENT DOOM FROM ITS OWN UNSTABLE CORE.

HIS LOYAL LIEUTENANT AND LOVER *URSA* AT HIS SIDE, GENERAL ZOD LED AN ILL-FATED *INSURRECTION* AGAINST THE KRYPTONIAN SCIENCE COUNCIL FOR THE GOOD OF THE PEOPLE TOO SMUG AND FOOLISH TO BELIEVE JOR-EL'S THEORIES.

ZOD FOUND THE IRONY MOST BITTER WHEN JOR-EL WAS NAMED AS HIS JAILER.

FOR CRIMES AGAINST KRYPTON, THE GENERAL AND HIS CO-CONSPIRATORS WERE SENTENCED TO IMPRISONMENT WITHIN THE *PHANTOM ZONE.* THE TERM OF THEIR CAPTIVITY: *LIFE.*

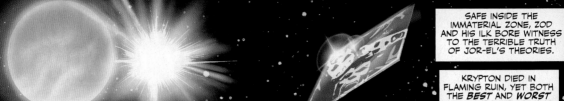

SAFE INSIDE THE IMMATERIAL ZONE, ZOD AND HIS ILK BORE WITNESS TO THE TERRIBLE TRUTH OF JOR-EL'S THEORIES.

KRYPTON DIED IN FLAMING RUIN, YET BOTH THE *BEST* AND *WORST* OF IT SURVIVED IN WAYS NO ONE IMAGINED.

PRIOR TO KRYPTON'S END, A PHANTOM ZONE PROJECTOR *MISHAP* TRANSPORTED *FORT ROZZ* INTO THE ZONE.

SOMEHOW RETAINING ITS PHYSICAL INTEGRITY AND ALLOWING ANYONE WHO SET FOOT INSIDE IT MATERIAL SUBSTANCE, THE PRISON WOULD BE A *BEACHHEAD* FOR ZOD'S RETURN.

A GOOD GENERAL KNOWS WHEN TO CHOOSE HIS BATTLES.

IF THERE IS NO KRYPTON LEFT TO SERVE, ZOD WILL FIND *ANOTHER* WORLD TO TAKE ITS PLACE.

AFTER ALL, THE GENERAL HAS HIS OWN SON--SIRED WITHIN THE PHANTOM ZONE-- TO CONSIDER.

AND SINCE JOR-EL DOES NOT SURVIVE TO FEEL HIS *VENGEANCE*...

THEN THE *SON* OF JOR-EL WILL *KNEEL* BEFORE ZOD!

Powers and Weapons:

LIKE ANY KRYPTONIAN UNDER THE RAYS OF A YELLOW SUN, GENERAL ZOD POSSESSES SUPER-ABILITIES: FLIGHT, NEAR-INVULNERABILITY, HEAT VISION AND OTHER SUPER-ENHANCED SENSES, SUPER-STRENGTH, AND SUPER-SPEED. A CUNNING MILITARY STRATEGIST, ZOD KNOWS HOW TO WIELD THESE NEWLY ACQUIRED POWERS TO WREAK MAXIMUM CARNAGE AS A ONE-MAN WEAPON OF MASS DESTRUCTION.

Essential Storylines:

- ACTION COMICS ANNUAL 10
- SUPERMAN: LAST SON

THE ORIGIN OF GRANNY GOODNESS

WRITER—SCOTT BEATTY
ARTIST—JON BOGDANOVE

LETTERER—TRAVIS LANHAM
COLORIST—HI-FI
EDITOR—ELISABETH V. GEHRLEIN

GRANNY GOODNESS CREATED BY JACK KIRBY

ON THE FIRE-POCKED SURFACE OF DISTANT APOKOLIPS, *EVERYONE* SERVES THE GREAT DARKSEID IN ONE WAY OR ANOTHER.

SOME DO SO WITH GREATER ZEAL THAN OTHERS.

SHOCK TROOPER GOODNESS HABITUALLY DEMONSTRATED THE IRONY IN HER NAMING.

AND WHEN SHE WAS AWARDED HER OWN WARHOUND TO TRAIN, GOODNESS CALLED THE BEAST *MERCY*...

SERVICE TO DARKSEID INVOLVES SACRIFICE EVEN DURING TRAINING EXAMINATIONS, BUT GOODNESS COULD NOT BRING HERSELF TO PUT DOWN HER BELOVED WARHOUND AS A TEST OF HER UNFLINCHING LOYALTY TO THE DREAD LORD OF APOKOLIPS.

...FOR MERCY IS WHAT ONE BEGGED IF CAUGHT BETWEEN TOOTH AND CLAW OF HER LOYAL HOUND.

INSTEAD, SHE DENIED THE EXAMINER MERCY.

DARKSEID SHOWED HIS BY GIVING HER A RARE SECOND CHANCE TO PROVE HER WORTH.

IN THE END, LIKE ANY WELL-TRAINED SERVANT ON APOKOLIPS, BOTH THE WARHOUND AND TROOPER GOODNESS PROVED LOYAL TO DARKSEID FIRST AND FOREMOST.

GOODNESS HAD DEMONSTRATED HER SKILL IN INSTILLING BLIND OBEDIENCE IN ANY CREATURE. SHE GRADUATED FROM THE WARHOUND KENNELS TO A PRISON ORPHANAGE WITHIN THE FILTHY SLUMS OF ARMAGETTO.

FREEDOM = DEATH
DEATH = FREEDOM

IN TIME, GRANNY GOODNESS SHOWED EVERY LAST PITIFUL POPPET IN HER CARE THAT NO ONE GETS OUT *SCOT-FREE*...

...AT LEAST NOT WITHOUT A FEW REMINDERS OF GRANNY'S LESS-THAN-TENDER MERCY.

THOSE MOST WILLING TO BEND TO GRANNY'S WILL BECAME HER *FEMALE FURIES*, WARRIOR WOMEN LOYAL TO GRANNY *FIRST*, BUT DARKSEID *FOREMOST*.

GRANNY NOW NUMBERS AMONG DARKSEID'S ELITE, HER REWARD FOR SO MANY UNINTERRUPTED YEARS OF UTTER RUTHLESSNESS.

POWERS AND WEAPONS:

In her youth, Granny Goodness was one of Darkseid's most feared shock troopers. She remains a robust and formidable fighter despite her age. Her patience thin, Granny punishes any misbehavior with her searing energy-gauntlets.

ESSENTIAL STORYLINES:

- Jack Kirby's MISTER MIRACLE
- SECRET ORIGINS OF SUPER-VILLAINS 80-page Giant 1
- AMAZONS ATTACK
- COUNTDOWN 1-4

THE ORIGIN OF GORILLA GRODD

WRITER--SCOTT BEATTY

ARTIST--ARTHUR ADAMS

LETTERER--TRAVIS LANHAM

COLORIST--HI-FI

EDITOR--ELISABETH V. GEHRLEIN

EVOLUTION IS *OVERRATED.*

THOSE BELIEVING THAT *GORILLA GORILLA GRAUERI* HAD *DEAD-ENDED* ON THE EVOLUTIONARY LADDER NEVER ENCOUNTERED A PREVIOUSLY ISOLATED TROOP OF LOWLAND APES IN EQUATORIAL AFRICA.

A CLOSE ENCOUNTER WITH A DOWNED EXTRATERRESTRIAL SPACECRAFT IMBUED THE GORILLAS WITH INTELLIGENCE FAR BEYOND THAT OF THEIR FELLOW SIMIANS, OR EVEN MAN FOR THAT MATTER.

AND FOR TWO APES IN PARTICULAR--KINDLY *SOLOVAR* AND BRUTISH *GRODD*--THE ALIEN'S GIFT INCLUDED A UNIQUE "FORCE OF MIND."

THUS ENDOWED, THE *SUPER-GORILLAS* SET TO WORK BUILDING A HAVEN FOR THEMSELVES AND THEIR ALIEN BENEFACTOR TO RIVAL ANY MAN-MADE METROPOLIS IN THE "CIVILIZED" WORLD.

EMBOLDENED BY HIS TRANSFORMATION, GRODD BIDED HIS TIME, WAITING FOR THE OPPORTUNITY TO SEIZE GREATER POWER.

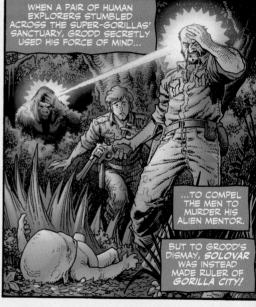

WHEN A PAIR OF HUMAN EXPLORERS STUMBLED ACROSS THE SUPER-GORILLAS' SANCTUARY, GRODD SECRETLY USED HIS FORCE OF MIND...

...TO COMPEL THE MEN TO MURDER HIS ALIEN MENTOR.

BUT TO GRODD'S DISMAY, *SOLOVAR* WAS INSTEAD MADE RULER OF *GORILLA CITY!*

FEARING MANKIND'S INFLUENCE WOULD BRING FURTHER BLOODSHED, THE SUPER-GORILLAS CLOAKED GORILLA CITY BEHIND AN IMPENETRABLE AND INVISIBLE *AURA-SCREEN* FOR DECADES TO FOLLOW.

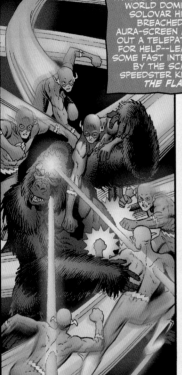

BUT WHEN GRODD USURPED GORILLA CITY'S THRONE AND THREATENED WORLD DOMINATION, SOLOVAR HIMSELF BREACHED THE AURA-SCREEN AND CAST OUT A TELEPATHIC CALL FOR HELP--LEADING TO SOME FAST INTERVENTION BY THE SCARLET SPEEDSTER KNOWN AS *THE FLASH.*

UNFORTUNATELY, IT WOULD NOT BE THE LAST TIME GRODD DECLARED *GORILLA WAR* UPON MANKIND.

ALTHOUGH AN ADMITTED SPECIESIST, THE EVIL SUPER-SIMIAN IS NOT ABOVE ALLYING HIMSELF WITH LESSER BEINGS--INCLUDING SO-CALLED HUMAN "SUPERVILLAINS"-- TO REALIZE HIS DREAM OF CREATING A SINGLE PAN-GLOBAL NATION...

...ALL CREATURES GREAT AND SMALL UNDER THE RULE OF *GRODD!*

POWERS AND WEAPONS:

GIFTED WITH SUPER-INTELLIGENCE AND FORMIDABLE PSYCHOKINETIC ABILITIES, GRODD CAN TRANSFER HIS CONSCIOUSNESS INTO THE BODIES OF OTHER CREATURES, TELEPATHICALLY CONTROL WEAKER MINDS, TRANSFORM MATTER TO A LIMITED EXTENT, AND PROJECT TELEKINETIC FORCE BEAMS. HE HAS DEVISED AN ARSENAL OF EXOTIC WEAPONS TO FURTHER HIS GOALS OF GLOBAL CONQUEST.

ESSENTIAL STORYLINES:

- THE FLASH 106
- JLAPE
- SUPERMAN/BATMAN: PUBLIC ENEMIES
- THE FLASH: ROGUES
- JLA: ULTRAMARINE CORPS
- SALVATION RUN

AFFILIATIONS:

- SECRET SOCIETY OF SUPER-VILLAINS
- SIMIAN SCARLET
- TARTARUS
- INJUSTICE LEAGUE

ARTHUR ADAMS
12-13-2007

THE ORIGIN OF GREEN ARROW

WRITER-MARK WAID
PENCILLER-SCOTT McDANIEL
INKER-ANDY OWENS
COLORIST-ALEX SINCLAIR
LETTERER-TRAVIS LANHAM
ASST. EDITOR-HARVEY RICHARDS
ASSOC. EDITOR-JEANINE SCHAEFER
EDITOR-MICHAEL SIGLAIN

OLIVER QUEEN, MILLIONAIRE PLAYBOY. HIS KEENEST SURVIVAL SKILL WAS HIS ABILITY TO MAKE A MARTINI LAST AN ENTIRE HOUR.

THAT LIFE OF LEISURE ENDED THE DAY HE FELL OFF A YACHT AND, CLINGING FOR FLOTATION TO A MOVIE PROP, WASHED ASHORE ONTO A DESERTED ISLAND.

QUEEN SURVIVED MONTHS OF SOLITUDE ONLY BY USING THAT PROP--A SIMPLE LONGBOW--TO HONE HIS ARCHERY AND HUNTING SKILLS TO PERFECTION--

--BUILDING IN HIMSELF A GRITTY SENSE OF SELF-RELIANCE HE WOULD OTHERWISE NEVER HAVE DISCOVERED.

BY THE TIME QUEEN FOUND HIS WAY HOME-- "COURTESY" OF SMUGGLERS USING THE ISLAND AS A HIDDEN BASE--HE'D ALREADY DECIDED THAT THERE WAS MORE TO LIFE THAN TUXEDOS AND SUPERMODELS.

HOOKED ON ADRENALINE AND ADVENTURE, QUEEN MADE HIMSELF THE COSTUMED DEFENDER OF STAR CITY, POURING HIS MILLIONS INTO GIMMICKED EQUIPMENT AND BATTLING THREATS BEYOND THE REACH OF THE ORDINARY LAW. HE HAD HIS FUN--

--BUT IT COST HIM HIS FORTUNE. OVERNIGHT, PENNILESS, QUEEN WENT FROM FIGHTING SUPER-VILLAINS TO BATTLING THE STREET CRIME AND SOCIAL INJUSTICE OUTSIDE HIS TENEMENT DOOR.

IT WAS THE FINAL TEMPERING HIS UPPER-CLASS SOUL REQUIRED.

GONE FOREVER WAS THE DILETTANTE HERO. IN HIS PLACE STOOD AN ARMED-AND-READY POLITICAL ACTIVIST--

--A PASSIONATE LEFT-WING CRUSADER AND URBAN AVENGER DEDICATED TO PROTECTING THE LESS FORTUNATE.

NOW HE DEFENDS STAR CITY IN BOTH HIS IDENTITIES. BY DAY, HE IS MAYOR OLIVER QUEEN--BY NIGHT, THE GREEN ARROW.

POWERS AND WEAPONS:

GREEN ARROW IS THE WORLD'S GREATEST ARCHER, A FORMIDABLE SWORDSMAN, AND A BARROOM BRAWLER OF THE HIGHEST CALIBER.

ESSENTIAL STORYLINES:

- MORE FUN COMICS 73, 89
- SHOWCASE PRESENTS THE GREEN ARROW
- GREEN ARROW: THE LONGBOW HUNTERS
- GREEN ARROW: QUIVER
- GREEN ARROW: THE ARCHER'S QUEST

THE ORIGIN OF GREEN LANTERN

MARK WAID · WRITER
IVAN REIS · PENCILS
OCLAIR ALBERT · INKS

ALEX SINCLAIR · COLORS
KEN LOPEZ · LETTERS
HARVEY RICHARDS · ASST. EDITOR
STEPHEN WACKER · EDITOR

CAPTAIN HAL JORDAN, U.S.A.F., MADE HIS REP AS THE MOST COURAGEOUS--AND MOST EXPENSIVE--TEST PILOT ALIVE.

LITTLE DID HE REALIZE HE'D SOON BE FLYING UNDER HIS OWN POWER.

SELECTED AMONG ALL EARTHMEN FOR HIS FEARLESSNESS AND HONESTY, JORDAN WAS SUMMONED TO A REMOTE LOCATION AND INTO THE REMAINS OF A CRASHED STARSHIP.

INSIDE, JORDAN FOUND A WOUNDED ALIEN, A MEMBER OF AN INTERGALACTIC PEACEKEEPING FORCE.

WITH HIS DYING BREATH, THE ALIEN PASSED HIS RING AND BATTERY OF POWER TO JORDAN--

--INDUCTING HIM INTO THE GREEN LANTERN CORPS, AGENTS OF THE GUARDIANS OF THE UNIVERSE.

AS A GREEN LANTERN, JORDAN USES HIS INCREDIBLE POWER RING TO PATROL AND DEFEND NOT ONLY OUR WORLD BUT ALL OF SPACE SECTOR 2814--

--PARTNERED FREQUENTLY WITH EARTH'S FELLOW LANTERN JOHN STEWART AND BACKED AS NEEDED BY CORPS MEMBERS FROM THROUGHOUT KNOWN SPACE AS THEY SHED THEIR LIGHT OVER THE DARKNESS OF EVIL AND CHAOS.

POWERS AND WEAPONS:

Green Lantern is armed with a ring the abilities of which are limited only by his imagination and will power.

Chiefly, the ring is used for antigravity, to unleash torrents of energy, to translate alien dialects and to create hard-light replicas of any shape. Though it has in the past been unable to affect yellow-colored objects, this impurity has since been overridden by Hal's will.

The ring must be periodically charged by contact with a Power Battery which, in turn, draws energy from the Guardians' Central Power Battery on the planet Oa.

ESSENTIAL STORYLINES:

GREEN LANTERN ARCHIVES
GREEN LANTERN: EMERALD DAWN
GREEN LANTERN: REBIRTH
GREEN LANTERN CORPS: RECHARGE

ALLIANCES:

Justice League of America, Green Lantern Corps

THE ORIGIN OF HARLEY QUINN

WRITER--SCOTT BEATTY
ARTIST--BRUCE TIMM
LETTERER--KEN LOPEZ
COLORIST--HI-FI
EDITOR--ELISABETH V. GEHRLEIN
HARLEY QUINN CREATED BY PAUL DINI AND BRUCE T

LOVE MAKES YOU DO *CRAZY* THINGS.

ASSIGNED TO PSYCHOANALYZE THE CLOWN PRINCE OF CRIME, *DR. HARLEEN QUINZEL* THOUGHT SHE COULD PLUMB THE DEPTHS OF THE JOKER'S MANIACAL PSYCHE AND PERHAPS CURE HIM.

INSTEAD, SHE FELL *MADLY* IN LOVE WITH HIM.

AND THEN SHE SHOWED THE ACE OF KNAVES JUST HOW FAR SHE WAS WILLING TO *COMMIT* TO THEIR RIBALD ROMANCE.

AS PROOF THAT HER FEELINGS WERE *CERTIFIABLE,* DR. QUINZEL HELPED HER "MISTAH J" ESCAPE FROM ARKHAM ASYLUM.

UNFORTUNATELY, THEIRS WAS A CLASSIC *LOVE/HATE* RELATIONSHIP:

HARLEY LOVED HER "PUDDIN"...

...BUT HE *HATED* HOW SHE CRAMPED HIS STYLE. SO HE FIRED HER OFF IN A MISSILE, WHICH WAS CERTAINLY NOT THE FIRST TIME HE SHOT HER.

LUCKILY FOR HARLEY, THE JOKER'S ROCKET FIZZLED. RIVAL ROGUE POISON IVY PROVIDED COMIC RELIEF, NURSING HARLEY BACK TO HEALTH WITH PLANT POTIONS THAT MADE THE CAPERING CLOWN GIRL EVEN MORE LIMBER.

THEIR PARTNERSHIP SHORT-LIVED, HARLEY DID SOLO STAND-UP HEISTS BETWEEN STINTS AT ARKHAM ASYLUM--

--AS A *PATIENT* THIS TIME.

HOWEVER, HARLEY WAS DEALT A DIFFERENT HAND WHEN SHE AIDED THE BATMAN IN TAKING DOWN THE NEW VENTRILOQUIST.

FREED FROM ARKHAM FOR HER GOOD BEHAVIOR, HARLEY IS BACK ON THE STRAIGHT AND NARROW PATH...

MOSTLY.

POWERS AND WEAPONS:

As a result of Poison Ivy's "treatment," Harley's strength and agility were increased dramatically, and she became immune to most toxins, including Joker-Venom. Like "Mistah J," Harley employs a variety of clown-themed gag weapons, including oversized pistols and mallets. Hyenas are her favorite pets.

ESSENTIAL STORYLINES:

- BATMAN: HARLEY QUINN
- HARLEY QUINN: PRELUDES AND KNOCK-KNOCK JOKES
- HARLEY AND IVY: LOVE ON THE LAM
- DETECTIVE COMICS 83 , 837
- COUNTDOWN TO FINAL CRISIS VOL. 1-4

THE ORIGIN OF
HAWKMAN
AND
HAWKGIRL

MARK WAID-WRITER
JOE BENNETT-PENCILS
RUY JOSE-INKS
ALEX SINCLAIR-COLORS
PAT BROSSEAU-LETTERS
HARVEY RICHARDS-ASST. EDITOR
STEPHEN WACKER-EDITOR

HAWKMAN AND
HAWKGIRL
CREATED BY
GARDNER FOX

CARTER HALL AND KENDRA SAUNDERS ARE DESTINED TO FALL IN LOVE.

AS PRINCE KHUFU AND HIS CONSORT, CHAY-ARA, THEY PERISHED CENTURIES AGO WHILE BATTLING AN EGYPTIAN SORCERER...

...ONLY TO BE REINCARNATED REPEATEDLY THROUGHOUT THE AGES, THEIR FATES FOREVER INTERTWINED.

AT ONE ANOTHER'S SIDE IN EACH LIFETIME, THEY FOUGHT IN THE SERVICE OF JUSTICE AND HONOR...

...EVENTUALLY, AT THE DAWN OF THE MODERN HEROIC AGE, THEIR SOULS FINDING ONE ANOTHER AGAIN AS CARTER AND SHIERA HALL--HAWKMAN AND HAWKGIRL.

IN THIS INCARNATION, HOWEVER, THEIR RELATIONSHIP TOOK A STUNNING TURN WHEN CARTER CHEATED THE CYCLE OF DEATH AND REBIRTH...

...AND SHIERA DIDN'T.

UNWILLING TO SEPARATE FROM CARTER, SHIERA'S SOUL HELD TO THIS LIFE BY INTERMINGLING WITH THAT OF HER GRANDNIECE, KENDRA SAUNDERS--BUT AT A TERRIBLE COST.

LIKE CARTER, KENDRA IS DRIVEN TO HEROISM--UNLIKE HIM, SHE HAS NO MEMORIES OF ANY PAST LIVES AND REBELS STRONGLY AGAINST HER FEELINGS TOWARD THIS MAN SHE SEEMS FATED TO LOVE.

AS APART AS OFTEN AS THEY ARE TOGETHER, THESE WINGED HUNTERS SOAR ABOVE ST. ROCH, LOUISIANA PROTECTING ITS CITIZENS FROM BIZARRE MENACES BOTH EARTH-BASED AND INTERGALACTIC.

WHETHER THEIR PASSION CAN SOMEDAY BE REKINDLED, HOWEVER...ONLY TIME WILL TELL.

POWERS AND WEAPONS:

The Hawks defy gravity using artificial wings and harnesses made of Nth Metal from the planet Thanagar.
Both are aggressive combatants skilled in ancient weaponry.

ESSENTIAL STORYLINES:

- Legend of the Hawkman
- JSA: Return of Hawkman
- Hawkman: Endless Flight

ALLIANCES:

Justice Society of America
Justice League of America

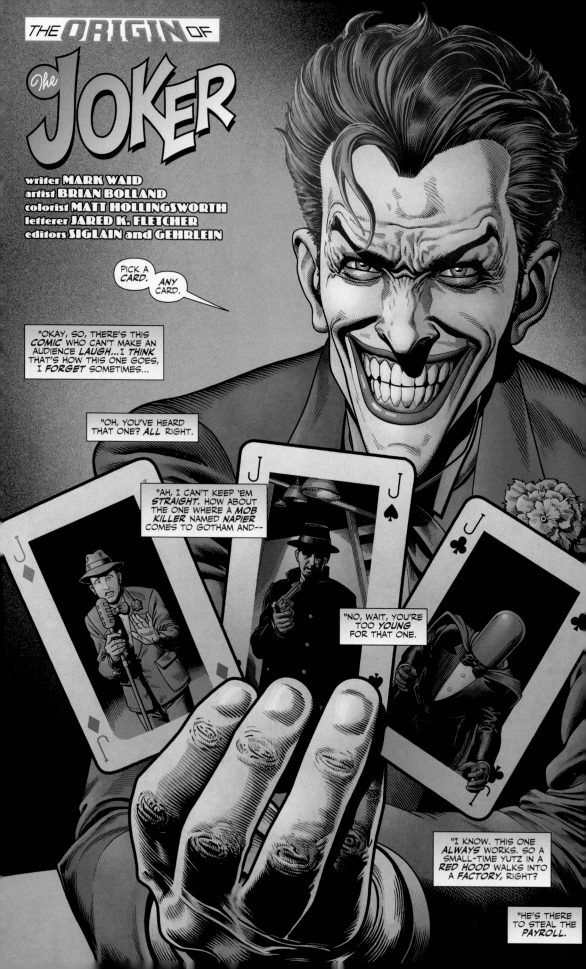

The ORIGIN of the JUSTICE LEAGUE AMERICA

writer **MARK WAID**
pencils **IVAN REIS**
inks **OCLAIR ALBERT**
colors **ALEX SINCLAIR**
letters **ROB LEIGH**
asst. editor **HARVEY RICHARDS**
assoc. editor **JEANINE SCHAEFER**
editor **MICHAEL SIGLAIN**

THEY HAD BEEN WATCHING.

THE WARRING LEADERS OF THE PLANET APPELLAX--HAVING MONITORED FROM AFAR THE END OF EARTH'S GOLDEN AGE OF HEROES--ASSUMED THEY WERE SAFE IN CLAIMING OUR NOW-UNDEFENDED WORLD AS THEIR ULTIMATE BATTLEGROUND.

A NEW GENERATION PROVED THEM WRONG.

DURING THE ALIENS' LONG TREK TO EARTH, NEW DEFENDERS HAD ARISEN, FAST CREATING THEIR OWN HEROIC LEGACY. TOGETHER, THEY REPELLED THE APPELLAXIAN INVASION.

EAGER TO CONTINUE WORKING AS A TEAM, DRAWING INSPIRATION FROM THE RETIRED JUSTICE SOCIETY, THESE "FRESHMEN HEROES" FORMED A LEAGUE OF THEIR OWN.

INITIALLY, BLACK CANARY, AQUAMAN, FLASH, GREEN LANTERN AND THE MARTIAN MANHUNTER FORMED THE GROUP'S CORE. BEFORE LONG, CO-FOUNDERS SUPERMAN, BATMAN AND WONDER WOMAN ASSUMED FULL MEMBERSHIP, AS WELL.

IN THE YEARS SINCE, ALMOST ALL OF EARTH'S CHAMPIONS HAVE AT ONE TIME OR ANOTHER HELD A PLACE ON THE ROSTER.

AMONG HEROES, THERE IS NO GREATER HONOR THAN BEING ASKED TO JOIN THE JUSTICE LEAGUE OF AMERICA.

FROM THEIR HEADQUARTERS IN WASHINGTON, DC, THE JLA SERVES AS MANKIND'S PREMIER PROTECTORS, EARTH'S FRONTLINE AGAINST THREATS TOO POWERFUL FOR ANY ONE HERO TO DEFEAT.

RED TORNADO

HAWKGIRL

BLACK CANARY

BLACK LIGHTNING

GEO-FORCE

GREEN LANTERN

RED ARROW

VIXEN

WONDER WOMAN

BATMAN

SUPERMAN

ESSENTIAL STORYLINES:

Writer – MARK WAID
Pencils – DON KRAMER
Inks – MICHAEL BAIR
Colors – ALEX SINCLAIR
Letters – ROB LEIGH
Asst. Editor – HARVEY RICHARDS
Assoc. Editor – JEANINE SCHAEFER
Editor – MICHAEL SIGLAIN

The Origin of the

JUSTICE SOCIETY AMERICA

THEY WERE THE FIRST SUPER-TEAM--ICONS OF THE GOLDEN AGE OF HEROES, BROUGHT TOGETHER TO PROTECT AMERICA DURING A TIME OF GLOBAL WAR.

AS THE JUSTICE SOCIETY, THEY SERVED MANKIND FOR MORE THAN A GENERATION BEFORE DISBANDING UNDER PRESSURE FROM A MISGUIDED GOVERNMENT.

GONE BUT NOT FORGOTTEN, THE JSA WAS EVENTUALLY SUMMONED OUT OF RETIREMENT BY THEIR SUCCESSORS, THE JUSTICE LEAGUE.

THE SOCIETY SOON FOUND THAT, WHEN IT CAME TO THEIR MOTIVES AND THEIR METHODS, THIS NEW ERA WAS MORE FORGIVING AND MORE ACCEPTING--

--BUT TIME ITSELF WAS NOT.

EVEN SUPER-HEROES AGE AND, AS YOUNGER HEROES JOINED THE JSA, THE MIGHT OF ITS ELDER STATESMEN GRADUALLY FLICKERED AND FADED.

SOME RETURNED TO CIVILIAN LIFE, OTHERS FELL IN BATTLE, AND THOSE WHO REMAINED PREPARED TO MARCH GRACEFULLY INTO TWILIGHT...

...BUT THE FIRES OF ANOTHER WORLD WAR REIGNITED THE JSA'S FIGHTING SPIRIT.

THE IMPACT THEIR HEROISM PROVIDED--THEIR KNOWLEDGE AND EXPERIENCE, WHICH RALLIED EARTH'S SOLDIERS AT A CRITICAL MOMENT-- GAVE THE SOCIETY A RENEWED SENSE OF PURPOSE.

DESPITE THEIR WEARINESS, FLASH, GREEN LANTERN AND WILDCAT REALIZED THEY HAD NO RIGHT TO ABANDON YOUNGER HEROES TO CAREERS OF GREAT POWER BUT LITTLE GUIDANCE.

TOGETHER, OPERATING FROM THEIR NEW HEADQUARTERS IN NEW YORK'S BATTERY PARK, THEY HAVE DEDICATED THEMSELVES TO RECRUITING AND TRAINING THE NEXT GENERATION OF CRIMEFIGHTERS.

CYCLONE

STAR-SPANGLED KID

AMAGE

ALAN SCOTT

POWER GIRL

OBSIDIAN

JAKEEM THUNDER & THUNDER-BOLT

STARMAN

SANDMAN

HOURMAN

JAY GARRICK

CITIZEN STEEL

LIBERTY BELLE

WILDCAT

DR. MID-NITE

MR. TERRIFIC

ESSENTIAL STORYLINES:
- Justice Society Volume One
- All-Star Comics Archives
- JSA: Justice Be Done

THE ORIGIN OF KILLER FROST

WRITER--SCOTT BEATTY
PENCILLER--JAMAL IGLE

INKER--KEITH CHAMPAGNE
LETTERER--TRAVIS LANHAM
COLORIST--HI-FI
EDITOR--ELISABETH V. GEHRLEIN

THE MAXIM GOES THAT NO TWO SNOWFLAKES ARE *EVER* EXACTLY ALIKE.

DR. CRYSTAL FROST THOUGHT THE ACHIEVEMENT OF THE ARCTIC-BASED THERMAFROST GENERATOR WOULD THAW RELATIONS WITH HER UNREQUITED LOVE, *PROFESSOR MARTIN STEIN.*

BUT STEIN'S COOL RESPONSE TO FROST'S AMOROUS ADVANCES WAS *NOTHING* COMPARED TO THE CHILL SHE FELT AFTER ACCIDENTALLY LOCKING HERSELF INSIDE THE HYPER-COLD THERMAFROST CHAMBER.

FROZEN TO HER CORE, FRAGILE CRYSTAL BECAME FRIGID *KILLER FROST,* AN ICE MAIDEN DETERMINED TO HEAP A BLIZZARD OF SCORN UPON *EVERY* MAN WHO HAD EVER WRONGED HER...

...INCLUDING MARTIN STEIN, ONE-HALF OF THE FUSED HERO KNOWN AS *FIRESTORM.*

DRAWN TO HEAT SOURCES FOR SURVIVAL, KILLER FROST PURSUED THE FLAME-HAIRED NUCLEAR MAN TO HER OWN HYPOTHERMIC END...

...DESPITE ALL ATTEMPTS BY *DR. LOUISE LINCOLN,* CRYSTAL FROST'S FORMER PROTÉGÉ, TO REVERSE HER TRAGIC TRANSFORMATION.

DESPITE THE UNFAVORABLE ODDS OF IDENTICAL SNOWFLAKES EXISTING, DR. LINCOLN RECREATED THE THERMAFROST ACCIDENT AND MADE HERSELF INTO AN ICY REFLECTION OF HER MENTOR, MUCH TO FIRESTORM'S DISMAY.

LATER, LINCOLN TRADED WHAT REMAINED OF HER FRACTURED SOUL TO THE DEVILISH *NERON*.

MADE MORE POWERFUL THAN HER PREDECESSOR, AN EVEN DEADLIER KILLER FROST THREATENED TO BLANKET EARTH IN A NEW ICE AGE!

BUT NO ONE--NOT EVEN MR. FREEZE HIMSELF DURING A FROSTBITTEN FLING--WARMS THE COCKLES OF A COLD-HEARTED KILLER FROST LIKE FIRESTORM IN *ANY* INCARNATION.

AS AN ASSASSIN-FOR-HIRE, KILLER FROST RECENTLY PUT HER VICTIMS ON ICE FOR COLD HARD CASH BEFORE CHILLING OUT WITH LEX LUTHOR'S INJUSTICE LEAGUE AS ITS RESIDENT SNOW QUEEN.

Powers & Weapons:

KILLER FROST IS ABLE TO GENERATE TEMPERATURES AS LOW AS ABSOLUTE ZERO IN ORDER TO CREATE WHITEOUT BLIZZARDS OR ICICLE-LIKE MISSILES. SHE PREFERS TO FLASH-FREEZE HER VICTIMS, ENTOMBING THEM IN BLOCKS OF ICE.

Essential Storylines:

- FIRESTORM 3
- THE FURY OF FIRESTORM 20-21
- FIRESTORM THE NUCLEAR MAN: REBORN
- JUSTICE LEAGUE OF AMERICA 13-15

Affiliations:

- SECRET SOCIETY OF SUPER-VILLAINS
- SUICIDE SQUAD
- INJUSTICE LEAGUE

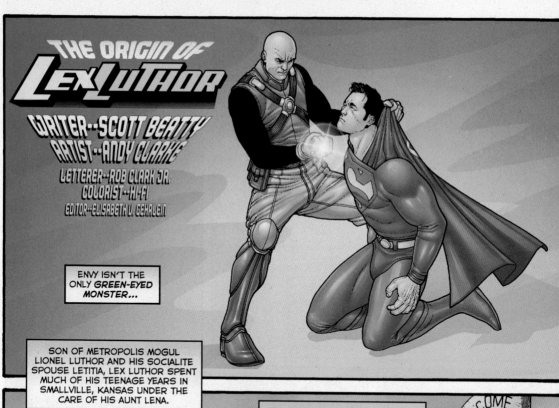

THE ORIGIN OF LEX LUTHOR

WRITER--SCOTT BEATTY
ARTIST--ANDY CLARKE
LETTERER--ROB CLARK JR.
COLORIST--HI-FI
EDITOR--ELISABETH V. GEHRLEIN

ENVY ISN'T THE ONLY *GREEN-EYED MONSTER*...

SON OF METROPOLIS MOGUL LIONEL LUTHOR AND HIS SOCIALITE SPOUSE LETITIA, LEX LUTHOR SPENT MUCH OF HIS TEENAGE YEARS IN SMALLVILLE, KANSAS UNDER THE CARE OF HIS AUNT LENA.

PERHAPS HIS PARENTS THOUGHT THAT FRESH MIDWESTERN AIR AND SMALLTOWN VALUES MIGHT CURE LEX OF HIS ANNOYING PROPENSITY FOR ALWAYS ACTING LIKE THE SMARTEST GUY IN THE ROOM.

THERE, LEX MIGHT EVEN FIND FRIENDS...

PETE, LANA, CLARK, AND LEX (SMILING AS USUAL!)

...ALBEIT *RELUCTANTLY,* AS WAS HIS WAY.

OR HE MIGHT JUST LEAVE IN HASTE UNDER A CLOUD OF RUMOR AND SUSPICION--

--FRIENDLESS AND ENVIOUS OF OTHERS' LIVES ONCE MORE.

ELSEWHERE, HE MIGHT PROVE TO EVERYONE THAT HE REALLY *WAS* THE SMARTEST GUY IN THE ROOM.

ANY ROOM.

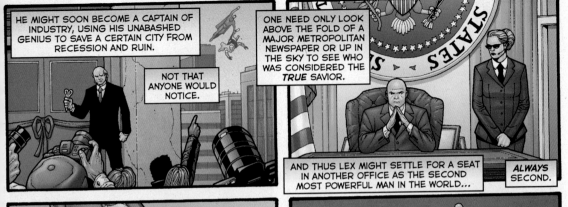

HE MIGHT SOON BECOME A CAPTAIN OF INDUSTRY, USING HIS UNABASHED GENIUS TO SAVE A CERTAIN CITY FROM RECESSION AND RUIN.

NOT THAT ANYONE WOULD NOTICE.

ONE NEED ONLY LOOK ABOVE THE FOLD OF A MAJOR METROPOLITAN NEWSPAPER OR UP IN THE SKY TO SEE WHO WAS CONSIDERED THE *TRUE* SAVIOR.

AND THUS LEX MIGHT SETTLE FOR A SEAT IN ANOTHER OFFICE AS THE SECOND MOST POWERFUL MAN IN THE WORLD...

ALWAYS SECOND.

THE GREEN-EYED MONSTER ISN'T ALWAYS ENVY.

IT MIGHT BE AN ADDICTION TO SOMETHING GREATER THAN POWER ITSELF.

IT MIGHT BE THE REALIZATION THAT EVERY FRIENDSHIP HAS ITS PRICE...

THAT MEN OF STEELY RESOLVE ALWAYS FIND A WAY TO UNDERMINE LEX'S AMBITIONS.

OR IT MIGHT BE THAT LEX LUTHOR--

--INARGUABLY SUPERMAN'S GREATEST FOE--

--JUST WON'T SETTLE FOR BEING *POWERLESS.*

BIZARRO #1

Powers & Weapons:

ONE OF THE SMARTEST MEN ON EARTH, LEX LUTHOR HAS DEMONSTRATED THAT HIS GENIUS KNOWS NO BOUNDS, WHETHER ENGAGED IN SCIENTIFIC BREAKTHROUGH OR CRIMINAL ENTERPRISE. IN THE PAST HE HAS EMPLOYED A HIGH-TECH WARSUIT OF HIS OWN DIABOLICAL DESIGN IN BATTLE WITH THE MAN OF STEEL. LEX BRIEFLY GAINED SUPERPOWERS VIA AN ARTIFICIAL EXO-GENE DEVELOPED IN HIS "EVERYMAN PROJECT." ANY LINGERING AFTEREFFECTS REMAIN TO BE SEEN.

Essential Storylines:

- SUPERMAN: PRESIDENT LEX
- SUPERMAN/BATMAN: PUBLIC ENEMIES
- VILLAINS UNITED
- 52
- SUPERMAN: UP, UP, AND AWAY

THE ORIGIN OF LOBO

MARK WAID-WRITER
KEITH GIFFEN-PENCILS
JACK JADSON-INKS
THE HORIES-COLORS
NICK J. NAPOLITANO-LETTERS
HARVEY RICHARDS-ASST. EDITOR
STEPHEN WACKER-EDITOR
LOBO created by
KEITH GIFFEN & ROGER SLIFER

YEARS AGO, ON THE BLISSFUL, UTOPIAN PLANET CZARNIA, A CHILD WAS BORN.

BEFORE HE EVEN LEFT THE DELIVERY ROOM, HE WAS NAMED LOBO.

IN THE LANGUAGE OF THE KHUNDIAN EMPIRE, IT'S A NAME THAT TRANSLATES THUSLY:

"HE WHO DEVOURS YOUR ENTRAILS AND THOROUGHLY ENJOYS IT."

EVEN AS A CHILD, LOBO'S STRENGTH AND SAVAGERY WERE ECLIPSED ONLY BY HIS GENERAL BASTICHNESS.

BY THE TIME HE WAS SIXTEEN, A FOUNTAIN OF MALICE, HE'D ELIMINATED HALF THE CZARNIAN RACE.

BY SEVENTEEN, HE STOPPED SCREWING AROUND.

IT'S A LUCKY MAN WHO TURNS HIS HOBBY INTO HIS PROFESSION.

BURSTING WITH ENTREPRENEURIAL SPIRIT, LOBO ESTABLISHED HIMSELF AS THE UNIVERSE'S MOST ACCOMPLISHED GENOCIDAL BADA$$ BY ELIMINATING HIS ENTIRE RACE.

UTTERLY ALONE, THE LAST CZARNIAN THEN WENT ABOUT FINDING OTHERS--

--FOR A FEE.

HIS BRAWLING, BOOZING, GAMBLING AND WOMANIZING NEVER GOT IN THE WAY OF THE BOUNTY-HUNTING SKILLS FOR WHICH HE BECAME KNOWN GALAXYWIDE. IF YOU NEEDED SOMEONE LOCATED, LOBO WAS YOUR MAN.

HOWEVER, TO MAKE A DEAL WITH LOBO IS TO HAVE THE DEVIL HIMSELF CALL YOU A CHUMP. LOBO'S PERSONAL CODE OF HONOR REQUIRES HIM TO OBEY ONLY THE STRICT LETTER OF AN AGREEMENT, AND IF YOU ENGAGE HIM IN ANY WAY, YOU HAVE ONLY YOURSELF TO BLAME FOR THE OUTCOME.

BECAUSE HE WILL DESTROY ANYTHING IN HIS PATH. ANYTHING. (EXCEPT SPACE DOLPHINS, OF WHICH HE IS INEXPLICABLY PROTECTIVE.)

TO LEARN THAT LOBO IS AFTER YOU IS TO KNOW THE SUDDEN EXPERIENCE OF SPONTANEOUS DEFECATION.

ENJOY IT.

IT WILL BE YOUR LAST MOMENT OF WARMTH IN THIS LIFETIME.

POWERS AND WEAPONS:

Lobo possesses exceptional strength and fortitude and cannot be killed--not just because he's tough, but because both Heaven and Hell have thrown him out and barred his return.

He is the universe's most gifted tracker, able to traverse the vacuum of space effortlessly and find any target given enough time-- and, being virtually immortal, time is always on Lobo's side.

ESSENTIAL STORYLINES:

- LOBO'S GREATEST HITS
- LOBO: PORTRAIT OF A BASTICH

THE ORIGIN OF MARTIAN MANHUNTER

Writer – MARK WAID
Artist – TOM MANDRAKE
Colorist – ALEX SINCLAIR
Letterer – PAT BROSSEAU
Asst. Ed – HARVEY RICHARDS
Assoc. Ed – JEANINE SCHAEFER
Editor – MICHAEL SIGLAIN

MARTIANS FELL BY THE SCORE, THEIR ENTIRE RACE BURNED AWAY BY A TELEPATHIC PLAGUE.

ONLY MANHUNTER J'ONN J'ONZZ LIVED TO EXACT JUSTICE FROM THE GENOCIDAL MADMAN RESPONSIBLE--

--BUT JUSTICE DIDN'T BRING BACK J'ONN'S WIFE OR BABY DAUGHTER. FOR THE FIRST TIME IN HIS LIFE, J'ONN WAS ALONE WITH HIS THOUGHTS.

UTTERLY ALONE.

THAT WOULD CHANGE.

RANDOMLY, J'ONN WAS PLUCKED FROM MARS TO EARTH BY THE ENERGIES OF DR. SAUL ERDEL'S EXPERIMENTAL TELEPORTER--

--WHICH, POWERED BY UNSTABLE RADIATION ON THE VOLATILE ZETA SCALE, CONSUMED ITSELF VIOLENTLY AND IMMEDIATELY.

IN THE AFTERMATH OF THE BLAST, J'ONN USED HIS SHAPE-SHIFTING ABILITIES TO CALM ERDEL WITH A MORE HUMAN APPEARANCE, BUT IT WAS TOO LATE.

THE SHOCK OF J'ONN'S ALIENNESS COMBINED WITH THE LOSS OF HIS LIFE'S WORK

LOST ON AN UNFAMILIAR PLANET, FEARFUL OF SIMILAR REACTIONS BY OTHER EARTHLINGS, J'ONN CLOAKED HIMSELF IN THE IDENTITY OF "JOHN JONES," COLORADO POLICE DETECTIVE--

--THE FIRST OF MANY SUCH ALTER EGOS HE WOULD MAINTAIN IN ORDER TO PASS FREELY AMONG US.

YEARS LATER, ONCE THE JUSTICE LEAGUE OF AMERICA MADE ITS DEBUT, J'ONN FOUND A NEW KINSHIP.

J'ONN BELIEVED THAT THE JLA'S ENDORSEMENT EARNED HIM EARTH'S TRUST, AND HE BEGAN TO RELAX HIS GUARD.

IN DOING SO, HOWEVER, HE HAS REPEATEDLY CURSED HIMSELF BY IGNORING HIS NATIVE HERITAGE.

RECENTLY, HE HAS RE-EMBRACED HIS MARTIAN FORM IN HOPES OF DRAWING OTHERS TO HIM. FOR DECADES, HE HAS BELIEVED HIMSELF TO BE THE LAST LIVING MARTIAN.

HE IS MISTAKEN.

POWERS AND WEAPONS:

Flight, super-strength, near-invulnerability, enhanced speed, invisibility, telepathy, shape-shifting, and "Martian vision," which allows Jonn the ability to see through solid objects and over great distances and emit heat energy from his eyes. Jonn is vulnerable to flame.

ESSENTIAL STORYLINES:

• JLA: Year One
• Justice League of America #144
• Formerly Known as the Justice League
• Countdown to Infinite Crisis

THE ORIGIN OF THE METAL MEN

writer MARK WAID
artist DUNCAN ROULEAU
colorist ALEX SINCLAIR
letterer PHIL BALSMAN
asst. editor HARVEY RICHARDS
assoc. editor JEANINE SCHAEFER
editors WACKER & SIGLAIN

UNDER THE TUTELAGE OF FAMED FUTURIST T.O. MORROW, *DR. WILL MAGNUS* BECAME THE WORLD'S FOREMOST AUTHORITY ON *ELEMENTICS*--

--THE SYNTHESIS OF *CHEMISTRY* AND *ROBOTIC SCIENCE.*

MAGNUS'S LEGENDARY BREAKTHROUGH WAS THE INVENTION OF THE *RESPONSOMETER*--

--A MICROCOMPUTER THAT COULD ANIMATE PURE METALS, TURNING LIFELESS SUBSTANCES INTO HUMANOIDS CAPABLE OF *INDEPENDENT THOUGHT.*

EACH OF MAGNUS'S "METAL MEN" DEMONSTRATE NOT ONLY POWERS, REFLECTIVE OF THEIR CHEMICAL PROPERTIES, BUT–SURPRISINGLY–PERSONALITIES TO MATCH.

MERCURY IS VOLATILE, *PLATINUM* IS GLAMOROUS, STUTTERING *TIN* FEELS EXPENDABLE, AND SO ON...

...BUT ALL OF THEM SHARE, AT THEIR CORE, THEIR CREATOR'S NOBILITY.

HEROIC BY NATURE, THE METAL MEN SPECIALIZE IN DEFENDING EARTH FROM THE UNIQUE MENACE OF CUTTING-EDGE SCIENCE GONE WRONG...

...OFTEN SACRIFICING THEIR "LIVES" WITH THE FAITH THAT THEIR BELOVED "DOC" CAN SOMEHOW SALVAGE THEIR RESPONSOMETERS AND REBUILD THEM...AS HE HAS HUNDREDS OF TIMES BEFORE.

POWERS AND WEAPONS:

Each of the Metal Men has abilities defined by his or her chemical makeup. Gold is infinitely ductile; Mercury is liquid at room temperature; Iron is durable; Lead is strong and protective; Tin is remarkably malleable and tough; and Platinum (or "Tina"), who thinks of herself as Magnus's true love, is particularly resistant to chemical, electrical or temperature-based attacks. The Metal Men alloy themselves as needed to combat specific threats.

ESSENTIAL STORYLINES:

- Metal Men Archives 1
- 52

The Origin of
METAMORPHO
The ELEMENT MAN

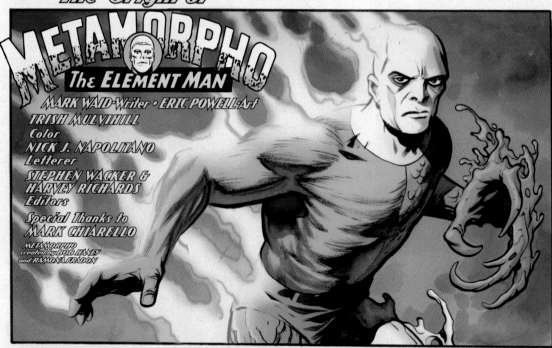

MARK WAID-Writer • **ERIC POWELL**-Art

TRISH MULVIHILL
Color

NICK J. NAPOLITANO
Letterer

STEPHEN WACKER &
HARVEY RICHARDS
Editors

Special Thanks to
MARK CHIARELLO

METAMORPHO
created by BOB HANEY
and RAMONA FRADON

YEARS AGO, REX MASON WAS A SOLDIER OF FORTUNE EXTRAORDINAIRE. ADAPTABLE TO ALL CULTURES AND CIRCUMSTANCES, NO TREASURE WAS BEYOND MASON'S REACH--

--SAVE THE HAND OF HEIRESS SAPPHIRE STAGG, WHOM MASON REFUSED TO MARRY UNTIL HE COULD AFFORD TO MATCH HER LIFESTYLE.

BELIEVING HE'D FOUND HIS BIG SCORE, MASON ACCEPTED A MISSION FROM SAPPHIRE'S FATHER, SIMON, TO UNEARTH THE FABLED *ORB OF RA* WITHIN THE PYRAMID OF *AHK-TON.*

MASON SUCCEEDED--

--ONLY TO HAVE IT STOLEN MOMENTS LATER BY SIMON'S JEALOUS ASSISTANT, *JAVA,* WHO SHARED HIS MASTER'S CONTEMPT FOR SAPPHIRE'S BELOVED.

LEFT FOR DEAD INSIDE THE PYRAMID, MASON WAS EXPOSED TO THE RADIATION OF AN ANCIENT METEOR BURIED THERE, A RADIATION THAT SAVED HIS LIFE--

--BUT LEFT HIM PERMANENTLY AND TRAGICALLY TRANSFORMED.

WHEN HE AWOKE, HE FOUND HIMSELF HIDEOUSLY ALTERED, THE CHEMICAL COMPONENTS OF HIS BODY SCRAMBLED AND REMIXED INTO A FREAKISH FORM.

HARDLY HUMAN, MASON COULD BARELY HOLD HIMSELF TOGETHER-- LITERALLY. THE SLIGHTEST THOUGHT WOULD CAUSE HIM TO SHIFT EFFORTLESSLY FROM GAS TO SOLID TO LIQUID.

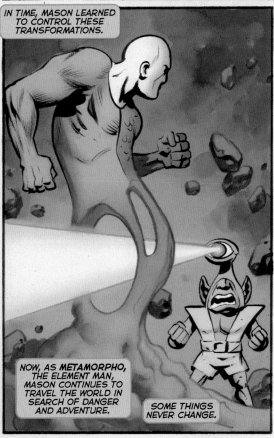

IN TIME, MASON LEARNED TO CONTROL THESE TRANSFORMATIONS.

NOW, AS METAMORPHO, THE ELEMENT MAN, MASON CONTINUES TO TRAVEL THE WORLD IN SEARCH OF DANGER AND ADVENTURE.

SOME THINGS NEVER CHANGE.

POWERS AND WEAPONS:

Metamorpho can transform himself into any element or compound found within the human body, from a fluorine cloud to an iron-cobalt battering ram.

The only object that can weaken the Element Man is the Orb of Ra--a vulnerability Simon Stagg uses to great advantage.

ESSENTIAL STORYLINES:

· Showcase Presents
· Metamorpho: Year One

THE ORIGIN OF MONARCH

Writer-SCOTT BEATTY
Artist-SCOTT KOLINS
Colorist-HI-FI Letterer-KEN LOPEZ
Editor-ELISABETH V. GEHRLEIN

IN EVERY MONARCHY THERE IS A LINE OF *SUCCESSION.*

MONARCH THE FIRST WAS *HANK HALL*--THE HERO *HAWK*--WHO EMBRACED DESPOTISM AFTER HIS PARTNER DOVE WAS MURDERED BY HALL'S OWN POWER-MAD FUTURE SELF.

MONARCH'S TIME-SPANNING REIGN OF TERROR WAS OPPOSED BY THE QUANTUM-LEAPING *WAVERIDER,* WHOSE POWERS HALL USURPED BEFORE CASTING ASIDE MONARCH'S ARMOR TO BECOME THE VILLAINOUS *EXTANT.*

UNFORTUNATELY, MONARCH'S ARMOR WOULD NOT REMAIN EMPTY FOR LONG.

THE METALLIC SECOND SKIN OF HEROIC *CAPTAIN ATOM* WAS ARMOR UNTO ITSELF, BUT IT OFFERED LITTLE PROTECTION WHEN HE WAS MAROONED ON AN EARTH NOT HIS OWN.

THERE, CAPTAIN ATOM ENCOUNTERED A WORLD WHOSE HEROES WERE FEARED AND LACKED CONTROL OVER THEMSELVES AND THEIR GODLIKE ABILITIES.

LIKE A PASSING STORM, CAPTAIN ATOM LEFT THAT EARTH CHANGED AND RETURNED TO HIS OWN PLANE WITH A RADICAL "WORLD-VIEW." PERHAPS HE WOULD HAVE EMBARKED ON A DIFFERENT PATH HAD HE NOT BEEN GRIEVOUSLY INJURED IN THE CHEMO-SCARRED RUINS OF BLÜDHAVEN.

TO PREVENT FURTHER CATASTROPHE CAUSED BY THE QUANTUM ENERGIES SEEPING FROM CAPTAIN ATOM'S DAMAGED SKIN, THE *ATOMIC KNIGHTS* SEALED HIM WITHIN THE RECOVERED ARMOR OF MONARCH.

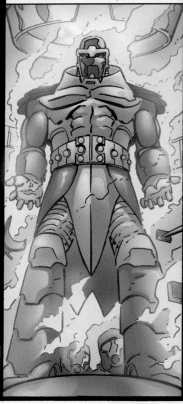

HIS ABILITIES ENHANCED BUT HIS CONTROL OVERWHELMED, CAPTAIN ATOM BECAME THE VERY THING HE FEARED AND FOUGHT ON THAT ALTERNATE EARTH.

HE REPAID THE KNIGHTS' KINDNESS BY DESTROYING WHAT LITTLE REMAINED OF BLÜDHAVEN BEFORE EMBRACING HIS FUTURE AS THE ONE *TRUE* MONARCH...

...AN UNDISPUTED LEADER WILLING TO CONFRONT THE 52 INCOMPETENT MONITORS AND ANYONE ELSE WHO WOULD ALLOW CHAOS TO PROLIFERATE THROUGHOUT THE MULTIVERSE...

...AND IN THE END CREATE ONE UNIFIED AND ORDERLY *UNI*VERSE UNDER HIS ABSOLUTE CONTROL!

POWERS AND WEAPONS:

With the powers of Captain Atom augmented by his futuristic armor, Monarch can manipulate the Quantum Field to wield great strength, manipulate antigravity, emit focused radioactive blasts, and travel at will between universes via The Bleed. Monarch now commands a vast war machine, capable of laying waste to entire worlds if need be, ready to fulfill his ultimate agenda -- unraveling the Multiverse to create one indivisible universe.

ESSENTIAL STORYLINES:

· ARMAGEDDON 2001
· ARMAGEDDON: THE ALIEN AGENDA
· CAPTAIN ATOM: ARMAGEDDON
· CRISIS AFTERMATH: THE BATTLE FOR BLÜDHAVEN
· COUNTDOWN

THESE ARE THE COLD HARD FACTS...

FROSTBITE, THE FREEZING DEATH OF LIVING TISSUE, OCCURS AT TEMPERATURES BELOW 32 DEGREES FAHRENHEIT.

HOWEVER, THE HEART CAN ENDURE MUCH *COLDER.*

TO SAVE HIS BELOVED WIFE NORA FROM A TERMINAL MALADY, GOTHCORP SCIENTIST VICTOR FRIES EXPERIMENTED IN *CRYOGENICS* TO PRESERVE NORA UNTIL SHE MIGHT BE CURED.

BUT AN ACCIDENTAL PLUNGE IN HIS OWN *SUPER-COOLANT* CONCOCTIONS DID MORE THAN CHILL VICTOR TO THE BONE.

HIS BODY CHEMISTRY IRREVOCABLY ALTERED, *MR. FREEZE*--AS HE NOW CALLED HIMSELF-- COULD ONLY SURVIVE SEALED WITHIN A SPECIALLY DESIGNED ENVIRONMENT SUIT THAT KEPT HIS BODY IN A PERMANENT STATE OF *HYPOTHERMIA.*

VICTOR WAS UNDERSTANDABLY VEXED WHEN GOTHCORP CUT THE FUNDING NECESSARY TO KEEP NORA SAFELY ON *ICE.*

AND ANY HOPE FOR NORA'S RECOVERY SHATTERED INTO A MILLION LITTLE PIECES WHEN, WHILE BATTLING A BATMAN INVESTIGATING A FLURRY OF UNTIMELY DEATHS AMONG GOTHCORP EXECUTIVES...

...VICTOR INADVERTENTLY FIRED HIS *FREEZE GUN* AT HER CRYO-CHAMBER.

THE ORIGIN OF MR. FREEZE

WRITER--SCOTT BEATTY
PENCILLER--THOMAS DERENICK
INKER--WAYNE FAUCHER
LETTERER--TRAVIS LANHAM
COLORIST--HI-FI
EDITOR--ELISABETH V. GEHRLEIN

IT HAS BEEN SAID THAT REVENGE IS A DISH BEST SERVED COLD.

FOR THE BATMAN AND HIS ALLIES, FREEZE WOULD HAVE IT NO OTHER WAY...

THAT IS, UNTIL A WELL-INTENTIONED BATGIRL HELPED FREEZE IMMERSE NORA'S REASSEMBLED CORPSE IN A LIFE-RESTORING *LAZARUS PIT* PROVIDED BY THE TREACHEROUS NYSSA, DAUGHTER OF RA'S AL GHUL.

NORA RETURNED TO LIFE, BUT HER LONG-DORMANT MIND WAS AS *BROKEN* AS HER BODY ONCE WAS.

ABSORBING THE PIT'S ALCHEMY INTO HER SCORCHING SKIN, NORA EMERGED LITERALLY *BURNING* WITH MADNESS AND THE POWER TO RAISE THE DEAD.

NOW FREEZE COULD NEVER EVER TOUCH THE WIFE HE SO LOVED.

HIS OWN FROZEN HEART BROKEN BEYOND REPAIR, THE *COLDEST* MR. FREEZE YET ENCOUNTERED LEAVES A WARY BAT-FAMILY WITH A SINGLE, SEARING QUESTION...

HOW *LOW* CAN HE GO?

POWERS AND WEAPONS:

Highly intelligent, Mr. Freeze has abandoned all other scientific pursuits except for perfecting the temperature-maintaining efficiency of his cryo-suit, which keeps him alive, and improving the deadly effectiveness of his freeze gun, which super-cools any ambient moisture in the air, encasing its target in a thick cocoon of ice.

ESSENTIAL STORYLINES:
- Batman 121
- Batman: Mr. Freeze
- Batman: Snow
- Batgirl 69-70

AFFILIATIONS:
- Secret Society of Super-Villains
- Injustice League of America

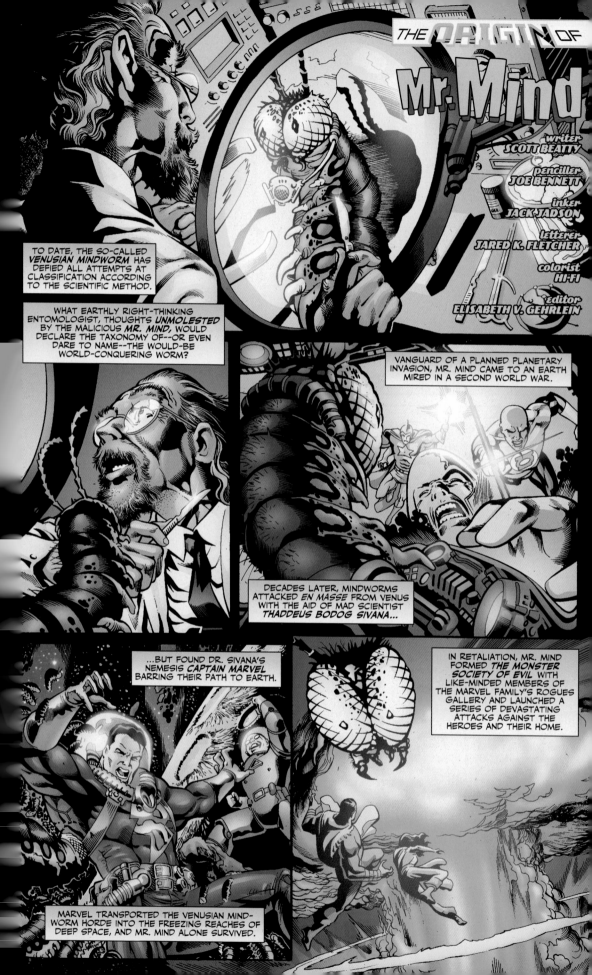

THE ORIGIN OF Mr. Mind

writer
SCOTT BEATTY

penciller
JOE BENNETT

inker
JACK JADSON

letterer
JARED K. FLETCHER

colorist
HI-FI

editor
ELISABETH V. GEHRLEIN

TO DATE, THE SO-CALLED *VENUSIAN MINDWORM* HAS DEFIED ALL ATTEMPTS AT CLASSIFICATION ACCORDING TO THE SCIENTIFIC METHOD.

WHAT EARTHLY RIGHT-THINKING ENTOMOLOGIST, THOUGHTS *UNMOLESTED* BY THE MALICIOUS *MR. MIND*, WOULD DECLARE THE TAXONOMY OF--OR EVEN DARE TO NAME--THE WOULD-BE WORLD-CONQUERING WORM?

VANGUARD OF A PLANNED PLANETARY INVASION, MR. MIND CAME TO AN EARTH MIRED IN A SECOND WORLD WAR.

DECADES LATER, MINDWORMS ATTACKED *EN MASSE* FROM VENUS WITH THE AID OF MAD SCIENTIST *THADDEUS BODOG SIVANA*...

...BUT FOUND DR. SIVANA'S NEMESIS *CAPTAIN MARVEL* BARRING THEIR PATH TO EARTH.

IN RETALIATION, MR. MIND FORMED *THE MONSTER SOCIETY OF EVIL* WITH LIKE-MINDED MEMBERS OF THE MARVEL FAMILY'S ROGUES GALLERY AND LAUNCHED A SERIES OF DEVASTATING ATTACKS AGAINST THE HEROES AND THEIR HOME.

MARVEL TRANSPORTED THE VENUSIAN MIND-WORM HORDE INTO THE FREEZING REACHES OF DEEP SPACE, AND MR. MIND ALONE SURVIVED.

FOLLOWING FURTHER MISADVENTURES, MR. MIND CAME INTO THE POSSESSION OF DR. SIVANA, WHO BOMBARDED HIS ONE-TIME PARASITIC PARTNER WITH EXPERIMENTAL *SUSPENDIUM* PARTICLES, TRIGGERING MR. MIND'S LONG-DELAYED *METAMORPHOSIS*.

LITTLE DID SIVANA KNOW THAT MR. MIND WAS LESS A WORM THAN A *MAGGOT*.

THE MINDWORM WEAVED A TELEPORTING CHRYSALIS AND BEAMED HIMSELF INTO BOOSTER GOLD'S COMPUTERIZED COMPANION *SKEETS*...

...THE PERFECT COVER FOR MR. MIND'S ULTIMATE TRANSFORMATION INTO THE HORRIBLE *HYPERFLY!*

NO LONGER SUSTAINED BY BRAIN WAVES ALONE, MR. MIND GORGED UPON TIME AND SPACE IN A FEEDING FRENZY.

AND WITH EVERY FLAP OF HIS HYPERFLY WINGS, ONCE IDENTICAL WORLDS WERE IRREVOCABLY CHANGED...

...THUS RECREATING A *MULTIVERSE* OF FIFTY-TWO DIVERGENT EARTHS!

FORTUNATELY, BOOSTER GOLD, SUPERNOVA, AND RIP HUNTER THWARTED THE HYPERFLY'S INFESTATION OF THE TIME/SPACE CONTINUUM...

...BY REVERSING MR. MIND'S METAMORPHOSIS...

...AND RETURNING HIM TO RIGHT WHERE HE STARTED...

...A SPECIMEN JAR IN THE LAB OF DR. SIVANA.

THERE THE MINDWORM WAITS TO TURN ONCE MORE...

Powers & Weapons:

DESPITE HIS MINUSCULE SIZE, MR. MIND IS A TELEPATH OF THE HIGHEST ORDER AND PERHAPS THE MOST INTELLIGENT MEMBER OF HIS SPECIES. THOSE UNDER MR. MIND'S MENTAL THRALL ARE BLISSFULLY UNAWARE THAT THEIR THOUGHTS ARE BEING CONSUMED BY THE VORACIOUS VENUSIAN MINDWORM. HIS METAMORPHOSIS INTO A "HYPERFLY"--SINCE REVERSED--MADE MR. MIND NEARLY (AND BRIEFLY) OMNIPOTENT.

Essential Storylines:

- THE POWER OF SHAZAM! 15-17, 38-41
- JSA: BLACK REIGN
- 52

THE ORIGIN OF MR. MXYZPTLK

Writer
SCOTT BEATTY

Artist
KYLE BAKER

Letterer
KEN LOPEZ

Editor
ELISABETH V. GEHRLEIN

YOU LIKE ME! YOU *REALLY* LIKE ME!

'COURSE, YOU WOULDN'T KNOW IT AFTER SEEING ME KIDNAPPED AND TORTURED FOR THE LAST TWENTY PAGES!*

MAYBE I SHOULDA JUST STAYED BACK ON *ZRFFF*, WHERE OUR SCIENCE IS SO SOPHISTICATED IT LOOKS LIKE *SORCERY* TO YOU THREE-DIMENSIONAL RUBES!

TOODLES, SUCKERS!

*DELIGHT AS MXY TAKES IT ON THE CHIN THROUGHOUT PAGES 1-20 OF THIS VERY ISSUE! --ED.

BUT THERE'S MORE FUN TO BE HAD ON EARTH THAN BACK IN THE *FIFTH DIMENSION*, ESPECIALLY WITH A MARK LIKE SUPERMAN!

I JUST *LOOOOOVE* GIVING HIM THE BUSINESS, 'CAUSE THE MAROON OF STEEL IS POWERLESS AGAINST MY MAGICAL MOJO!

AND EVERY SO OFTEN I DON'T MIND *MIXING* IT UP WITH SUPEY'S OTHER PALS, LIKE *THE PRANKSTER* OR MY FELLOW CHROME-DOME *LEX LOSER.*

BURMA-SHAVE...

BUT HOWEVER I APPEAR, YOU CAN REST ASSURED THAT SUPERMAN IS IN FOR AN *IMPISHLY* BAD TIME OF FOUR-COLOR FUN...

UNLESS, OF COURSE, HE CAN TRICK ME INTO SAYING MY NAME *BACK*--

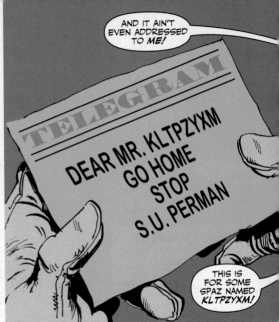

POWERS AND WEAPONS:

With near limitless magical powers at his command, Mr. Mxyzptlk can bend reality to his every whim. Thankfully, all of his magical mischief is restored to normal once Mxy is tricked into saying his name backwards, which forces him to return to Zrfff for 90 days.

ESSENTIAL STORYLINES:

- SUPERMAN 30
- SUPERMAN 131
- SUPERMAN: WHATEVER HAPPENED TO THE MAN OF TOMORROW?
- SUPERMAN: KRISIS OF THE KRIMSON KRYPTONITE
- SUPERMAN: EMPEROR JOKER

The Origin of MR. TERRIFIC

Writer · WAID
Artist · VAN SCIVER
Color · SINCLAIR
Letters · LEIGH
Asst. Editor · RICHARDS
Assoc. Editor · SCHAEFER
Editor · SIGLAIN

"NO JUSTICE," THEIR FATHER ALWAYS SAID.

MICHAEL HOLT WAS A CHILD PRODIGY WITH AN ASTRONOMICAL I.Q. AND A NATURAL ATHLETICISM THAT WOULD TAKE HIM WHEREVER HE WANTED TO GO.

HIS OLDER BROTHER, JEFFREY, WAS BORN SEVERELY RETARDED AND DIED AT FIFTEEN WITHOUT EVER KNOWING ANYTHING BUT MICHAEL'S LOVE.

IT WASN'T FAIR.

MICHAEL GREW UP AN OLYMPIC DECATHLETE AND SCHOLAR, ACCUMULATING DOCTORATES AND DEGREES, AMASSING A PERSONAL FORTUNE--

--BUT NEVER FINDING A PURPOSE UNTIL HE MET HIS WIFE, PAULA.

SHE DIED IN A FREAK ACCIDENT.

IT WASN'T FAIR.

PAULA HOLT

Peace In The Valley

WONDERFUL WIFE and BEST FRIEND

HE'D MAKE IT FAIR.

MICHAEL CONTEMPLATED LEAVING AN UNJUST WORLD HE'D GROWN TO HATE--

--BUT IN THAT MOMENT OF DECISION, THE MEMORY OF JEFFREY AND PAULA'S STRENGTH TURNED HIS BITTERNESS INTO RESOLVE.

THE WORLD WASN'T FAIR?

MICHAEL REDEDICATED HIS INTELLECT AND RESOURCES TOWARD THE PURSUIT OF JUSTICE IN ALL ITS FORMS.

CODE-NAMED **MR. TERRIFIC** AFTER A LEGENDARY HERO OF SIMILAR ORIGIN, MICHAEL NOW DIVIDES HIS TIME AS CHAIRMAN OF THE JUSTICE SOCIETY OF AMERICA--

--AND AS A MEMBER OF ONE OF THE ELITE ROYALS OF CHECKMATE, AN INTERNATIONAL INTELLIGENCE ORGANIZATION SWORN TO MAINTAIN THE BALACE OF WORLD POWER.

POWERS AND WEAPONS:

Mr. Terrific, the third-smartest man alive, is a master of martial arts and of several medical and scientific fields. He employs "T-spheres" of his own invention--floating robotic globes that project holograms and laser grids, serve as cameras and data links, and aid in assault. His special mask cloaks him from all forms of electronic detection.

ESSENTIAL STORYLINES:

- JSA: All-Stars

ALLIANCES:

- JSA
- Checkmate

THE ORIGIN OF NIGHTWING

Mark Waid...Writer   George Pérez...Art

Alex Sinclair...Colors   Phil Balsman...Letters

Harvey Richards...Asst. Editor

Stephen Wacker...Editor

Nightwing created by
Marv Wolfman and George Pérez

GOTHAM CITY WAS ONLY A ONE-NIGHT STOP FOR HALY'S CIRCUS. MANAGEMENT IGNORED THE MOB'S REQUEST FOR PROTECTION MONEY...

WELCOME TO THE ALL-STAR HALY CIRCUS

...UNTIL THE FLYING GRAYSONS "FELL" FROM THEIR TRAPEZE.

WHILE THE REST OF THE AUDIENCE SCREAMED IN TERROR, BRUCE WAYNE RELIVED THE TRAUMA OF A MURDERED FAMILY THROUGH THE EYES OF THE GRAYSONS' SON, DICK.

RECOGNIZING THE BOY'S PAIN, WAYNE ADOPTED THE ORPHAN AS HIS WARD...AND THE DARK KNIGHT BEGAN TRAINING HIS FIRST SQUIRE.

AS ROBIN, THE LAUGHING YOUNG DAREDEVIL THRIVED UNDER BATMAN'S GUIDANCE, BECOMING AN EXPERT CRIMEFIGHTER IN HIS OWN RIGHT.

AND, AS ALL BOYS MUST, HE EVENTUALLY GREW UP AND FLEW FROM THE NEST.

HAVING LEFT THE ROBIN IDENTITY BEHIND, DICK GRAYSON--ACROBAT, DETECTIVE, ADVENTURER-- PATROLS THE STREETS OF NEW YORK CITY AS NIGHTWING.

UNLIKE HIS FORMER MENTOR, HOWEVER, NIGHTWING ENTERS EACH AND EVERY FIGHT WITH A LOOMING UNCERTAINTY.

GRAVE CELESTIAL FORCES BEYOND OUR KEN HAVE INFORMED HIM THAT HIS SURVIVAL IN THE MULTIVERSE'S RECENT CRISIS WAS NEITHER EXPECTED NOR FORETOLD...AND THAT HIS ULTIMATE FATE IS YET TO BE DETERMINED.

POWERS AND WEAPONS:

The world's greatest acrobat, Nightwing is a master of combat styles. His bulletproof costume contains a number of hidden utility belt devices, chief among them a grappling line, stylized shurikens, and shatterproof escrima fighting sticks for close-quarters battle.

Even as a boy, Nightwing was uncommonly bright and mature for his age, and his ability to read people makes him not only an amazing detective but a team leader without equal, a trait not even his famed mentor shares.

ESSENTIAL STORYLINES:

· DETECTIVE COMICS 38
· ROBIN: YEAR ONE
· NIGHTWING: YEAR ONE
· TEEN TITANS: THE JUDAS CONTRACT

ALLIANCES:

Outsiders

DESPITE WHAT ASTROPHYSICISTS BELIEVE, THE UNIVERSE IS DEFINED NEITHER BY DIMENSION NOR BY SPACE...

...BUT BY *COLOR.*

THE ORIGIN OF PARALLAX

WRITER-*SCOTT BEATTY*
PENCILLER-*IVAN REIS*
INKER-*OCLAIR ALBERT*
LETTERER-*ROB CLARK JR.*
COLORIST-*HI-FI*
EDITOR-*ELISABETH V. GEHRLEIN*

YELLOW HAS ALWAYS BEEN THE COLOR OF *FEAR.*

SINCE CREATION BURST FORTH IN THE BIG BANG, LITTLE BLUE BEINGS HAVE MAINTAINED *ORDER.*

MILLENNIA AGO ON DISTANT OA, THE SELF-APPOINTED *GUARDIANS OF THE UNIVERSE* IMPRISONED THE PHYSICAL EMBODIMENT OF FEAR WITHIN THEIR GREAT CENTRAL BATTERY OF POWER.

BY THE GUARDIANS' GRAND DESIGN, BLUE AND YELLOW MADE GREEN, THE COLOR OF *COURAGE* AND THE MOST IMPORTANT QUALIFICATION FOR ENLISTMENT IN THE GUARDIANS' GREEN LANTERN CORPS.

BEINGS WITHOUT FEAR, THE GREEN LANTERNS WOULD THUS BELIEVE THE GUARDIANS' LITTLE WHITE LIE THAT THEIR ASTOUNDING POWER RINGS' VULNERABILITY TO YELLOW WAS A *"NECESSARY IMPURITY."*

BUT ASK ANY CORPS MEMBER--PAST OR PRESENT--AND HE, SHE, OR IT WILL TELL YOU THE SIMPLE TRUTH OF IT:

YELLOW IS THE COLOR OF *EVIL.*

SINCE TIME IMMEMORIAL, THE INFECTION OF FEAR HAS LED INEXORABLY TO VIOLENCE...

AND IN TURN, VIOLENCE FEEDS INSATIABLE FEAR.

MADDENED BY GRIEF OVER THE DESTRUCTION OF HIS BELOVED COAST CITY, GREEN LANTERN *HAL JORDAN* DESTROYED BOTH BLUE AND GREEN, UNDOING THE GUARDIANS AND THEIR CORPS IN ORDER TO ACQUIRE THE ENERGY NECESSARY TO MAKE THINGS RIGHT.

INSTEAD, HAL MADE HIMSELF A VESSEL FOR THE POWER OF FEAR.

AT LAST, FEAR HAD A NAME: *PARALLAX.*

TO REDEEM THE SINS OF PARALLAX, HAL PREVENTED EARTH'S FINAL NIGHT BY KINDLING ITS EXTINGUISHED SUN WITH ALL HIS EMERALD ENERGIES.

BUT FEAR COULD NOT WIN OUT IN A MAN ONCE BRANDED AS UNDENIABLY *FEARLESS.*

IN DEATH, HAL ASCENDED TO ANOTHER POST AS HOST FOR *THE SPECTRE.*

UNFORTUNATELY, THE FEAR ENTITY HAD GRAFTED ITSELF ONTO HAL'S VERY SOUL, AND EVEN GOD'S SPIRIT OF VENGEANCE WAS POWERLESS AGAINST AN EVIL SO PRIMAL.

HAL WAS FINALLY CLEAVED FROM PARALLAX WITH THE HELP OF HIS OLDEST AND MOST TRUSTED FRIENDS.

AND, THUS POSSESSED, HAL JORDAN UNLEASHED VIOLENCE IN A VAIN ATTEMPT TO TURN BACK TIME AND RESTORE COAST CITY TO LIFE.

HIS REBIRTH BROUGHT WITH IT A RESURRECTED GREEN LANTERN CORPS...

...AS WELL AS THE REVELATION OF THE *TRUE* POWER BEHIND FEAR'S RETURN: SINESTRO, ITS MOST *DEVOTED* DISCIPLE.

FUELING THE FEAR-DRIVEN *SINESTRO CORPS*, PARALLAX NOW RESIDES WITHIN THE ONE GREEN LANTERN *NOT* BORN FEARLESS.

AND IF THE GREATEST GREEN LANTERN BARELY ESCAPED THE CLUTCHES OF PARALLAX, WHAT CHANCE DOES KYLE RAYNER HAVE TO ESCAPE A FUTURE PAINTED ENTIRELY IN *YELLOW?*

Powers & Weapons:

FEAR LEADS TO VIOLENCE, WHICH IN TURN LEADS TO GREATER FEAR, AN ENDLESS LOOP OF TERROR AND DESTRUCTION FEEDING PARALLAX AND FUELING THE YELLOW ENTITY'S SEEMINGLY LIMITLESS POWER. WHERE A GREEN LANTERN'S POWER RING CAN GIVE EMERALD SUBSTANCE TO ANYTHING ITS WEARER IMAGINES, PARALLAX BRINGS TO GILDED LIFE THAT WHICH ITS VICTIMS FEAR MOST.

Essential Storylines:

- GREEN LANTERN: EMERALD TWILIGHT
- GREEN LANTERN: REBIRTH
- GREEN LANTERN: SINESTRO CORPS WAR

THE ORIGIN OF THE PENGUIN

WRITER—SCOTT BEATTY
PENCILLER—SCOTT MCDANIEL
INKER—ANDY OWENS
LETTERER—TRAVIS LANHAM
COLORIST—HI-FI
EDITOR—ELISABETH V. GEHRLEIN

OSWALD CHESTERFIELD COBBLEPOT SUFFERED TWO KINDS OF BULLIES AS A CHILD.

THE FIRST WAS HIS OVERPROTECTIVE AND OVERBEARING WIDOWED MOTHER, WHO WAS CONVINCED THAT, WERE OSWALD EVER CAUGHT IN A DOWNPOUR WITHOUT AN UMBRELLA, HE WOULD PERISH FROM PNEUMONIA LIKE HIS FATHER.

Cobblepot's Aviary
EXOTIC
~~RDS~~ & PETS

WITH HIS BEAKLIKE NOSE, PAUNCHY BELLY, AND OMNIPRESENT UMBRELLA, OSWALD WAS THUS THE EASIEST OF TARGETS FOR SCHOOLYARD TAUNTS.

UNFORTUNATELY, NICKNAMES LIKE "OSWALD THE PENGUIN" STUCK LIKE TARRED FEATHERS...

...AND FLOCKING WITH THE BIRDS OF HIS MOTHER'S PET SHOP, HIS ONLY TRUE FRIENDS, DID LITTLE TO CHANGE OSWALD'S PECULIAR IMAGE.

EVENTUALLY, THE PENGUIN NEEDED *OTHER* BIRDS TO MAKE HIM FEEL BETTER ABOUT HIMSELF.

WEALTH AND POWER HAVE A WAY OF SMOOTHING THE RUFFLED FEATHERS OF TROUBLED YOUTH.

A LIFE OF CRIME, HOWEVER, CAN BE A GILDED CAGE...

ESPECIALLY WHEN OSWALD'S FEATHERED FETISHES MADE HIS FELONIES ALL TOO PREDICTABLE TO GOTHAM CITY'S WINGED PROTECTORS.

EVEN A FLIGHTLESS FOWL KNOWS WHEN TO STAY PERCHED SAFELY ON THE GROUND.

FROM HIS NEST IN *THE ICEBERG LOUNGE*, OSWALD COBBLEPOT ONCE DABBLED IN THE BLACK MARKET, WADDLING HIS WAY THROUGH GOTHAM'S UNDERWORLD AS IT SUITED HIM.

THE PENGUIN PRESENTLY FLIES STRAIGHT, PECKING OUT A LEGITIMATE LIVING BY SELLING WHAT IS UNDENIABLY CRIMINALLY OVERPRICED MERCHANDISE. EVIDENTLY, AT THE ICEBERG, TWO-THIRDS OF THE MARKUP IS UNDER THE TABLE.

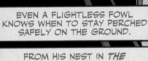

Powers & Weapons:

A DECEPTIVE AND DEVIOUS CRIMINAL MASTERMIND. THOUGH REMARKABLY AGILE FOR HIS SIZE AND BUILD, THE PENGUIN FINDS HAND-TO-HAND COMBAT BENEATH HIM. HE DOES, HOWEVER, EMPLOY A VARIETY OF WEAPONIZED UMBRELLAS FOR HIS OWN PERSONAL PROTECTION.

Essential Storylines:

- SECRET ORIGINS SPECIAL 1
- BATMAN: NO MAN'S LAND VOLUME 1
- BATMAN: BROKEN CITY

THE ORIGIN OF PLASTIC MAN

Writer – Mark Waid
Artist – Ethan Van Sciver
Colorist – Alex Sinclair
Letterer – Ken Lopez
Asst. Ed. – Harvey Richards
Assoc. Ed. – Jeanine Schaefer
Editor – Michael Siglain

Alias: Patrick "Eel" O'Brian, New York's slipperiest gangster.

Career highlight: attempting a multimillion-dollar heist from the Crawford Chemical Works.

Career lowlight: Failing.

In the escape, O'Brian was shot by a guard, his wound doused with an experimental acid.

Abandoned by his gang, O'Brian barely eluded capture before passing out on the grounds of a remote monastery.

Waking, O'Brian found that the acid had entered his blood and turned him into a shape-shifting, pliable man of rubber.

Moreover, the spiritual guidance of the monks led the Eel to a second, more profound transformation.

Recruited by a special branch of the F.B.I., he made a career out of collaring crooks--

He reformed, turning over a new leaf and adopting a new identity as **Plastic Man,** the long arm of the law.

WANTED
EEL O'BRIEN

--though, to Chief Branner's eternal exasperation, Eel O'Brien somehow managed to remain just out of Plas's grasp.

As O'Brian, he infiltrated criminal gangs; then, as "Plas," he brought his associates to justice.

O'Brian's known confederates are **Woozy Winks,** a bumbling but seemingly indestructible sidekick--

--and O'Brian's son, Ernie, who inherited his father's powers to become the crimefighter **Offspring.**

They are among the few who know of O'Brian's secret past.

NOT *ANYMORE,* PLASTIC CHUMP! THE UNDERWORLD'LL PAY *BIG MONEY* FOR A FILE LIKE DIS!

POWERS AND WEAPONS:

Plastic Man can stretch his body into any shape he can imagine, from the simple to the seemingly absurd. He can absorb and deflect small-arms fire without harm and can compress his mass to bowling-ball size or elongate it hundreds of yards. His most common vulnerabilities are to extreme temperatures.

ESSENTIAL STORYLINES:

PLASTIC MAN ARCHIVES
PLASTIC MAN 80-PAGE GIANT
PLASTIC MAN: ON THE LAM
PLASTIC MAN: RUBBER BANDITS

The Origin of Poison Ivy

Scott Beatty — Writer
Stephane Roux — Artist
Rob Clark Jr. — Letterer
Elisabeth V. Gehrlein — Editor

"Wallflower," they called her. "Shrinking violet."

Only *Jason Woodrue*--known in some circles as the *Floronic Man*--realized the pretty poison potential within the timid and unassuming *Dr. Pamela Isley.*

She only needed the proper care to *blossom*, and no one else had a green thumb like Woodrue.

He intended to grow Isley into a human/plant hybrid such as himself.

He never imagined that he had planted a thing such as *Poison Ivy*. Where Pamela Isley was not unattractive, Poison Ivy was undeniably *ravishing.*

She flowered with pheromone pollens that made males of all species bend to her will like a reed in the wind.

All except *one*, that is.

Ivy was *green* long before being environmentally friendly was in vogue.

But while Gotham City provided fertile ground to fund her eco-crusade, *The Batman* made sure Ivy didn't set down permanent roots on *his* soil.

For a time, Poison Ivy flitted like *pollen* blown on breezes to less-friendly climates.

And while she always did prefer the company of *men*...

...eventually, Ivy found a more kindred spirit who shared her love for all things the *color* of money.

But Ivy's toxic friendship with Harley Quinn has always branched back to a *terrarium* cell within dank and sunless Arkham Asylum.

More than a little *stir-crazy*, Poison Ivy currently finds her environmental cause less important than vengeful caprice. Left unchecked, a weed will *choke* itself.

And in the horrible *Harvest*--a hybrid horror germinated from all her victims--

--Ivy would have reaped what she had sown, if not for that one man resistant to her chlorophyll-laced charms.

Perhaps Batman believes she might one day turn over a new *leaf*...

...or maybe he knows that, at heart, Poison Ivy's just a *bad seed*.

Powers & Weapons:

HER BODY CHEMISTRY ALTERED BY WOODRUE'S MANIPULATION, IVY IS NOW MORE PLANT THAN HUMAN. SHE IS ABLE TO EXUDE A VARIETY OF FLORA-BASED POISONS AND MIND-NUMBING PHEROMONES. SHE HAS LIMITED CONTROL OVER CERTAIN PLANT LIFE, INCLUDING MONSTROUS HYBRIDS BIOENGINEERED BY IVY HERSELF.

Essential Storylines:

- BATMAN 181
- BATMAN: NO MAN'S LAND VOL. 3
- BATMAN: HARLEY AND IVY
- DETECTIVE COMICS 823

Affiliations:

THE INJUSTICE GANG OF THE WORLD
THE SECRET SOCIETY OF SUPER-VILLAINS
THE SUICIDE SQUAD

THE ORGIIN OF...

Power Girl

MARK WAID WRITER

ADAM HUGHES ART & COLOR

JARED K. FLETCHER LETTERER

HARVEY RICHARDS ASST. EDITOR

JEANINE SCHAEFER ASSOC. EDITOR

MICHAEL SIGLAIN EDITOR

WHEN THE DISTANT PLANET KRYPTON EXPLODED, TWO INFANT COUSINS WERE ROCKETED TO SAFETY.

ONE ARRIVED ON EARTH AS A CHILD AND GREW UP TO BE SUPERMAN.

THE OTHER-- KARA ZOR-L-- WAS HAMPERED BY A FAR SLOWER SHIP. KEPT ALIVE FOR DECADES IN SUSPENDED ANIMATION--

--SHE EVENTUALLY EMERGED ON EARTH FULLY GROWN AND EAGER TO LIVE THE KIND OF LIFE SHE'D ONLY BEEN ALLOWED TO DREAM ABOUT--

--AS POWER GIRL, SUPERMAN'S PARTNER AND CONFIDANTE.

IN TIME, HOWEVER, KARA LEARNED A DEVASTATING TRUTH BEHIND HER ORIGINS-- THAT SHE HAD BEEN BORN AND RAISED IN A PARALLEL UNIVERSE LATER ERADICATED IN A MULTIVERSAL CRISIS.

SHE HAS SINCE BEEN WELCOMED INTO THE DC UNIVERSE AS ITS SOLE SUPER-HEROIC SURVIVOR BY OTHERS WHO KNOW ALL TOO WELL WHAT IT'S LIKE TO LOSE FAMILY.

NOW, ALLIED WITH THE JUSTICE SOCIETY OF AMERICA, POWER GIRL HAS VOWED TO PROTECT HER ADOPTED HOMEWORLD FROM ANYTHING THAT MIGHT THREATEN IT.

SHE WILL NOT ENDURE THAT DEEP A LOSS AGAIN.

POWERS AND WEAPONS:

Energized by Earth's yellow sun, Power Girl possesses great strength, speed, invulnerability, and the ability to fly. Her super-senses include x-ray and telescopic vision, heat vision, super-hearing, and arctic breath. Like all Kryptonians, she is vulnerable to Kryptonite and is powerless under the rays of a red sun.

ESSENTIAL STORYLINES:

- Infinite Crisis
- Power Girl trade paperback

ALLIANCES:

Justice Society of America

THE ORIGIN OF PROMETHEUS

LEN WEIN WRITER
FEDERICO DALLOCCHIO ART & COLOR
PAT BROSSEAU LETTERS
ADAM SCHLAGMAN EDITOR
PROMETHEUS CREATED BY GRANT MORRISON

IF EVER ANYONE WAS QUITE LITERALLY **BORN** TO A LIFE OF CRIME, IT'S GOTTA BE THIS KID, HIS **TRUE IDENTITY** KNOWN ONLY TO HIMSELF...

HIS **PARENTS** WERE A MODERN-DAY **BONNIE AND CLYDE,** WHO TOOK THEIR SON ALONG ON THEIR YEARS-LONG CROSS-COUNTRY CRIME SPREE--

--AND ULTIMATELY **DIED** IN A HAIL OF POLICE BULLETS RIGHT BEFORE HIS EYES...

THE **TRAUMA** OF THAT MOMENT TURNED THE BOY'S HAIR PERMANENTLY **WHITE**--

--AND, OVER THEIR BULLET-RIDDLED BODIES, HE SWORE AN **OATH** TO DEVOTE HIS LIFE TO **ANNIHILATING** THE FORCES OF JUSTICE--

--THEN SET OUT TO DO PRECISELY **THAT.**

BUT BEING MERELY A KILLER WASN'T ENOUGH FOR THIS KID. HE NEEDED TO KNOW EVERYTHING.

SO HE SPENT THE REMAINDER OF HIS FORMATIVE YEARS TRAVELING THE WORLD, LEARNING HOW TO MAIM AND KILL IN A DOZEN DIFFERENT LANGUAGES--

--UNTIL, AT LAST, HIS JOURNEY LED HIM TO TIBET, IN SEARCH OF THE ANCIENT MYTHICAL KINGDOM OF EVIL KNOWN AS SHAMBALLA...

THERE, AT LAST, AN OLD LAMA FINALLY LED HIM DOWN TEN THOUSAND STEPS INTO THE **BOWELS** OF THE **TEMPLE MOUNTAIN**--

--WHERE THE ANCIENT ALIEN ENTITY CALLED **SHAMBALLA** STOOD WAITING.

DECLARING THE YOUNG MAN THE **CHOSEN ONE**, THE OLD LAMA GAVE HIM A KEY THAT COULD UNLOCK THE SPACES **BETWEEN DIMENSIONS**--

--AND THERE, IN THE SO-CALLED **GHOST ZONE**, THE YOUNG MAN BUILT HIS CROOKED HOME.

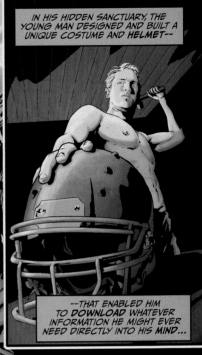

IN HIS HIDDEN SANCTUARY, THE YOUNG MAN DESIGNED AND BUILT A UNIQUE COSTUME AND HELMET--

--THAT ENABLED HIM TO **DOWNLOAD** WHATEVER INFORMATION HE MIGHT EVER NEED DIRECTLY INTO HIS MIND...

THEN, CONSIDERING HIMSELF MORE THAN SUITABLY **ARMED**, THE MAN NOW CALLED **PROMETHEUS** SET OUT TO DESTROY THE **JUSTICE LEAGUE**...

Powers and Weapons:

A MASTER OF MANY DIFFERENT FORMS OF MARTIAL ARTS, AND SKILLED WITH ALMOST EVERY KNOWN WEAPON, THE MAN CALLED PROMETHEUS HAS A CYBERNETIC IMPLANT WHICH ALLOWS HIM TO INSTANTLY DOWNLOAD ANY CONCEIVABLE DATA HE MIGHT NEED DIRECTLY INTO HIS BRAIN. HIS ARMORED UNIFORM PROTECTS HIM FROM MOST PHYSICAL HARM.

Essential Storylines:

- JLA: STRENGTH IN NUMBERS
- JLA: WORLD WAR III
- JUSTICE LEAGUE: CRY FOR JUSTICE
- FACES OF EVIL: PROMETHEUS #1

Affiliations:

- THE INJUSTICE GANG

the Origin of the Question

Mark Waid - Writer

Joe Bennett - Art

Alex Sinclair - Colors

Nick J. Napolitano - Letters

Harvey Richards - Asst. Edits

Stephen Wacker - Edits

ALL CHARLES VICTOR SZASZ EVER WANTED WAS ANSWERS.

WHO WERE HIS PARENTS? WHY DID THEY ORPHAN HIM? HOW WOULD HE SURVIVE A BRUTAL CHILDHOOD...

...AND WHAT KIND OF MAN WOULD HE BECOME?

AS "VIC SAGE," HE PURSUED A CAREER AS AN INVESTIGATIVE REPORTER IN THE CRIME-RIDDEN, FESTERING TOWN KNOWN AS HUB CITY.

IT WAS A FAIRLY EASY JOB. CORRUPTION IN HUB CITY WASN'T DIFFICULT TO FIND...

...THOUGH IT HATED LIKE HELL TO BE UNCOVERED. TO DO THAT JOB AND LIVE TO TELL ABOUT IT WOULD REQUIRE SOME MEASURE OF ANONYMITY.

ENTER ARISTOTLE RODOR, ONE OF SAGE'S FORMER COLLEGE PROFESSORS.

RODOR, DRAWING FROM THE EXTRACT OF THE GINGOLD PLANT AND FROM THE NOTES OF GOTHAM CRIMINAL BART MAGAN, HAD CREATED THE SUBSTANCE PSEUDODERM.

AS AN ARTIFICIAL SKIN, PSEUDODERM WAS DESIGNED FOR DRESSING WOUNDS.

WHEN EXPOSED TO A CERTAIN GAS, HOWEVER...

...IT MASKED SAGE'S APPEARANCE WHILE ALLOWING HIM TO SEE AND BREATHE NORMALLY.

AS REPORTER VIC SAGE, HE PURSUED THE FACTS.

AS THE QUESTION, HE PURSUES THE TRUTH.

POWERS AND WEAPONS:

Trained by Richard Dragon, one of the world's foremost martial artists, the Question is a supreme hand-to-hand combatant. He is also keenly observant and exceptionally intuitive as a detective.

ESSENTIAL STORYLINES:

- MYSTERIOUS SUSPENSE 1
- THE QUESTION (first series) 1-36
- BATMAN/HUNTRESS: CRY FOR BLOOD

THE ORIGIN OF RA'S AL GHUL

Writer~~Scott Beatty
Artist~~Cliff Chiang
Letterer~~Travis Lanham
Editor~~Elisabeth V. Gehrlein

THE TALE BEGINS THUS:

SINCE TIME IMMEMORIAL, MAN HAS SOUGHT THE MEANS TO EXTEND HIS LIFE PAST THE CONSTRICTIONS OF THE MORTAL COIL.

MANY CENTURIES AGO, A YOUNG PHYSICIAN LEARNED THE SECRET TO IMMORTALITY AND, AIDED BY HIS WIFE, USED IT TO SAVE THE LIFE OF A DYING PRINCE.

IMMERSED IN A "LAZARUS PIT," AN ALCHEMICAL FROTH OF ACIDS AND POISONS BREWED ABOVE ONE OF THE MANY MAGNETIC LEY LINES ENTWINING THE EARTH, THE PRINCE EMERGED FROM THE DEADLY BATH REJUVENATED...

...AND QUITE INSANE.

THOUGH HIS MADNESS WAS BUT TEMPORARY, THE PRINCE HELD NO ACCOUNT FOR THE SINS HE HAD WROUGHT AND CHOSE TO BURY THE TRUTH IN A SHALLOW, SANDY GRAVE.

TOO SHALLOW PERHAPS...

DETERMINED TO GRIEVE FOREVER-- BEYOND EVEN DEATH--THE PHYSICIAN ENDURED.

AND WHEN THE PRINCE FELL ILL YET AGAIN, HIS FATHER THE SULTAN BEGGED THE PHYSICIAN TO REPEAT HIS MAGIC.

ONLY THIS TIME THE REVENGE-MINDED PHYSICIAN MAY HAVE LEFT OUT A KEY INGREDIENT, SAVING THE SECRET OF ETERNAL LIFE FOR HIMSELF ALONE.

AS THE YEARS PASS, THE PHYSICIAN IS KNOWN BY DIFFERENT NAMES IN DIFFERENT ERAS AS HE AMASSES POWER AND WEALTH IN HIS CRUSADE TO CLEANSE THE PLANET OF MANKIND'S SCOURGE.

THE NAME HE PREFERS IS SPOKEN ONLY IN FEARFUL WHISPERS: RA'S AL GHUL...

THE DEMON'S HEAD, UNDISPUTED LEADER OF THE LEAGUE OF ASSASSINS.

AND FROM ANTIQUITY TO MODERNITY, HE HAS FOUND NO GREATER ADVERSARY THAN THE MAN HE CALLS SIMPLY **THE DETECTIVE**, WHOM RA'S AL GHUL ONCE CONSIDERED THE ONLY WORTHY SUCCESSOR TO INHERIT THIS SECRET EMPIRE UPON MARRIAGE TO HIS DAUGHTER **TALIA**.

UNABLE TO PRODUCE A SUITABLE MALE HEIR IN HIS MANY LIFETIMES, RA'S AL GHUL RAISED TWO DAUGHTERS GENERATIONS APART, ONE UNQUESTIONABLY **LOYAL**...

...THE OTHER **TREACHEROUS**.

SLAIN BY THE VENGEFUL **NYSSA**, RA'S AL GHUL DID NOT GO QUIETLY INTO THE GOOD NIGHT.

INSTEAD, HE WAS REBORN IN A RAPIDLY DETERIORATING IMITATION OF LIFE. HIS ONLY HOPE FOR TRUE REBIRTH WAS TRANSFERENCE OF HIS SOUL INTO THE BODY OF HIS GRANDCHILD **DAMIAN**, ILLEGITIMATE SON OF TALIA AND HER BELOVED BATMAN!

THOUGH DAMIAN WAS SPARED RA'S AL GHUL'S "INHERITANCE," THE **WHITE GHOST** WAS NOT. THE ALBINO SON OF RA'S AL GHUL, LONG KEPT SECRET FROM ALLIES AND ENEMIES ALIKE, BECAME THE VESSEL FOR THE INEVITABLE RESURRECTION OF THE DEMON'S HEAD.

AS WAS HIS WAY, THE DARK KNIGHT **DISAGREED**...

...AND NOW RA'S AL GHUL SERVES A **LIFE-SENTENCE** IN ARKHAM ASYLUM, KEPT SILENT AND IMMOBILE BY PRESENT-DAY MEDICINE.

BUT FOR A MAN WHO HAS ESCAPED DEATH'S CLUTCHES TIME AND AGAIN, SURELY STONE WALLS AND IRON BARS WILL NOT HOLD HIM FOR LONG.

POWERS AND WEAPONS:
In the centuries he has lived, Ra's al Ghul has become a master swordsman and ruthless fighter. He wields even greater power as leader of countless minions willing to go to their death in the name of the Demon's Head. His private bodyguard, always called Ubu, is chosen in a deathmatch between rival combatants vying for the position. Only Ra's al Ghul knows the alchemical formula to create a Lazarus Pit, a secret he jealously guards. He is a brilliant and cunning strategist and perhaps the greatest threat to human life on earth.

ESSENTIAL STORYLINES:
- Batman 232
- Batman: Son of the Demon
- Batman: Birth of the Demon
- Batman: Legacy
- Batman: Death and the Maidens
- The Resurrection of Ra's al Ghul

AFFILIATIONS:
- The League of Assassins

THE ORIGIN OF the Riddler

WRITER--SCOTT BEATTY   ARTIST--DON KRAMER
COLORIST--HI-FI   LETTERER--JARED K. FLETCHER
EDITOR--ELISABETH V. GEHRLEIN

AS A CHILD, EDWARD NASHTON'S LOVE FOR BRAIN-TEASERS WAS EXCEEDED ONLY BY HIS OWN OVERWHELMING DESIRE TO WIN AT ANY COST.

WHEN A GRADE SCHOOL TEACHER HELD A CONTEST AMONG EDDIE'S CLASSMATES TO SEE WHO COULD ASSEMBLE A PUZZLE THE FASTEST, HE EASILY OUTPACED HIS PEERS IN COMPLETING THE CHALLENGE.

CHESS

OF COURSE, EDDIE CHEATED.

AND IN THE GAME OF LIFE, CHANGING THE RULES TO ALWAYS TIP IN HIS FAVOR SET EDDIE ON A SLIPPERY SLOPE.

YOU LOSE

BLACK KEYS

GOTHAM CITY LIMITS

NEW YORK STAT

DRIVER LICENSE

NIGMA, EDWARD
1700 BROADWAY, #646
NEW YORK, NY 10019

SEX: M EYES: BL HT: 6-1

Edward Nigma

IT SHOULD COME AS NO SURPRISE, THEN, THAT EDDIE NASHTON'S DOWNWARD SLIDE PROPELLED HIM STRAIGHT INTO A LIFE OF CRIME.

HIS FIRST KNOWN ALIAS--E. NIGMA.

GET IT?

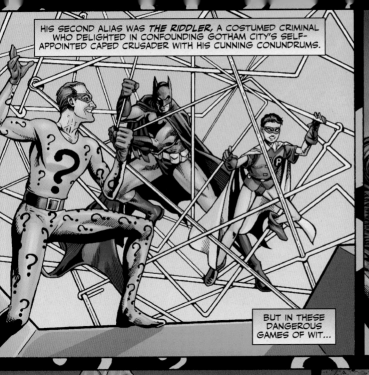

HIS SECOND ALIAS WAS *THE RIDDLER,* A COSTUMED CRIMINAL WHO DELIGHTED IN CONFOUNDING GOTHAM CITY'S SELF-APPOINTED CAPED CRUSADER WITH HIS CUNNING CONUNDRUMS.

...THE DARK KNIGHT HAS ALWAYS PROVED HIS SUPERIOR INTELLECT...

BUT IN THESE DANGEROUS GAMES OF WIT...

...AT LEAST UNTIL EDDIE FIGURED OUT HIS OPPONENT'S OWN NEARLY INSOLUBLE SECRET:

WHO IS BATMAN?

HOW LONG COULD THE RIDDLER KEEP THE ANSWER TO HIMSELF?

THAT WAS THE $64,000 QUESTION, WASN'T IT?

NOT LONG AGO, EDDIE UNFORTUNATELY SUFFERED A HEAD INJURY WITH A CONSOLATION PRIZE OF RANDOM MEMORY LOSS, INCLUDING HIS ONCE FAVORITE BAT-FACT.

NOW A RECOVERED AND REFORMED RIDDLER OFFERS HIS 'SKILLS' FOR PROFIT AS A PRIVATE INVESTIGATOR AND SECURITY CONSULTANT TO THE G.C.P.D.

TIME WILL TELL IF HIS NEW PROFESSION OR ALLEGED AMNESIA IS JUST ANOTHER SCHEME TO GET UNDER BATMAN'S COWL.

Powers & Weapons:

A BRILLIANT PUZZLER, THE RIDDLER IS CONVERSELY A POOR HAND-TO-HAND FIGHTER. HE WISELY RELIES ON HIRED MUSCLE, INCLUDING FEMMES FATALES AND FREQUENT ACCOMPLICES QUERY AND ECHO.
THE RIDDLER DOES LITTLE TO RESIST A DEEPLY ROOTED PSYCHOLOGICAL COMPULSION TO LEAVE CAREFULLY CONCOCTED CLUES TO HIS CRIMES FOLLOWING A HEIST, OR EVEN BEFORE HE HAS BROKEN THE LAW.

Essential Storylines:

- BATMAN: FEATURING TWO-FACE AND THE RIDDLER
- SECRET ORIGINS SPECIAL 1
- BATMAN: HUSH
- DETECTIVE COMICS 822, 828

0-555-CLUE CALL NOW! 1-800-555-CLUE CALL NO

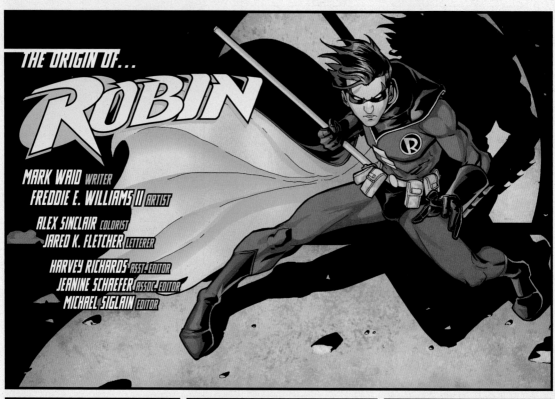

THE ORIGIN OF...
ROBIN

MARK WAID WRITER
FREDDIE E. WILLIAMS II ARTIST

ALEX SINCLAIR COLORIST
JARED K. FLETCHER LETTERER

HARVEY RICHARDS ASST. EDITOR
JEANINE SCHAEFER ASSOC. EDITOR
MICHAEL SIGLAIN EDITOR

THE EYES OF A FAN CAUGHT A MOMENT THE REST OF THE WORLD HAD OVERLOOKED.

TIM DRAKE-- AND TIM DRAKE ALONE-- HAD GROWN UP FASCINATED BY THE CAREER OF AN OBSCURE AND FORGOTTEN CHILD ACROBAT NAMED DICK GRAYSON--

--BUT WHEN TIM SAW BATMAN'S PARTNER ROBIN PERFORM GRAYSON'S SIGNATURE GYMNASTIC MOVES, SOMETHING CLICKED IN TIM'S MIND.

OVER THE NEXT FEW YEARS, TIM-- THROUGH A SERIES OF CLUES AND LUCKY BREAKS-- PROVED CONCLUSIVELY THAT GRAYSON WAS ROBIN...

...OR, RATHER, HAD BEEN.

BY THEN, DICK GRAYSON HAD "GRADUATED" TO BECOME NIGHTWING, RETIRING HIS ORIGINAL COSTUME. TO BATMAN, ROBIN HAD PROVED IRREPLACEABLE.

TIM DECIDED THAT WAS A MATTER OF OPINION.

THOUGH BATMAN RESISTED TIM'S EFFORTS TO JOIN HIS CRUSADE, TIM EVENTUALLY PERSEVERED AND WAS ALLOWED TO MAINTAIN THE IDENTITY--

--PROVIDED HE OVERCAME A GRUELING SERIES OF MENTAL AND PHYSICAL TRIALS THAT WOULD HAVE CHALLENGED THE DARK KNIGHT HIMSELF.

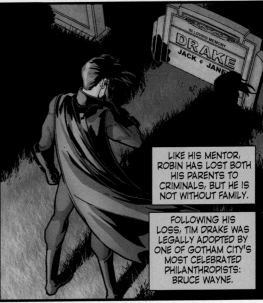

IN LOVING MEMORY
DRAKE
JACK & JANE

LIKE HIS MENTOR, ROBIN HAS LOST BOTH HIS PARENTS TO CRIMINALS, BUT HE IS NOT WITHOUT FAMILY.

FOLLOWING HIS LOSS, TIM DRAKE WAS LEGALLY ADOPTED BY ONE OF GOTHAM CITY'S MOST CELEBRATED PHILANTHROPISTS: BRUCE WAYNE.

POWERS AND WEAPONS:

Besides being a skilled detective and acrobat, Robin carries a mini-arsenal of devices including a collapsible bo staff, "R"-shaped shurikens, and a utility belt filled with gas pellets and other traditional bat-gadgets.

ESSENTIAL STORYLINES:

- BATMAN: YEAR THREE
- ROBIN: A HERO REBORN
- ROBIN: TRAGEDY AND TRIUMPH
- IDENTITY CRISIS

ALLIANCES:

Teen Titans

The ORIGIN of RED TORNADO

Writer - WAID - Layouts - JIMENEZ
Finishes - LANNING - Color - HI-FI - Letters - LEIGH
Asst. Editor - RICHARDS - Assoc. Editor - SCHAEFER
Editor - SIGLAIN

THOMAS OSCAR MORROW WAS A VISIONARY--AN INVENTOR QUITE LITERALLY ABLE TO SEE INTO THE FUTURE.

BY SAMPLING AND ADAPTING TOMORROW'S TECHNOLOGY, HE SPECIALIZED IN COMMITTING CRIMES SO SCIENTIFICALLY ADVANCED THAT THERE WERE NOT YET LAWS AGAINST THEM.

STILL, HE HAD MADE ENEMIES OF EARTH'S HEROES, SO HE INVENTED A DEFENDER--

--AN ANDROID DESIGNED TO INFILTRATE THE JUSTICE SOCIETY AND JUSTICE LEAGUE AND, AT MORROW'S COMMAND, DESTROY BOTH TEAMS FROM WITHIN.

IN THE RED TORNADO, MORROW HAD CREATED COLD MACHINE LIFE--BUT HE HAD NOT FORESEEN HOW HUNGRY IT WOULD BE FOR A SOUL.

POSSESSED BY ULTHOON, AN AIR ELEMENTAL FROM A DISTANT STAR, THE ANDROID BECAME SELF-ACTUALIZED--

--REBELLING AGAINST ITS MURDEROUS PROGRAMMING AND BECOMING A JUSTICE LEAGUER IN GOOD STANDING.

WITH BRUCE WAYNE'S HELP, THE SELF-DEPRECATING TORNADO CRAFTED THE IDENTITY "JOHN SMITH" IN AN ATTEMPT TO FEEL MORE "NORMAL."

OVER TIME, SMITH DREW TO HIM A FAMILY WHO RECOGNIZED HIS MACHINE ORIGINS BUT WHO BELIEVED IN THE MAN WITHIN.

MORROW HAD GIVEN THE RED TORNADO ITS SENTIENCE-- BUT ULTHOON GAVE IT MORALITY.

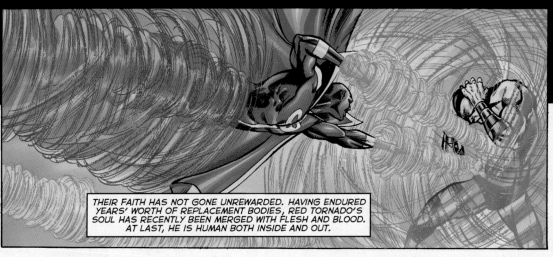

THEIR FAITH HAS NOT GONE UNREWARDED. HAVING ENDURED YEARS' WORTH OF REPLACEMENT BODIES, RED TORNADO'S SOUL HAS RECENTLY BEEN MERGED WITH FLESH AND BLOOD. AT LAST, HE IS HUMAN BOTH INSIDE AND OUT.

POWERS AND WEAPONS:

The Red Tornado can create cyclonic winds which, at maximum force, can level a building in seconds. His power allows him to fly through the air at great speed and to deflect approaching objects with ease.

ESSENTIAL STORYLINES:

- JUSTICE LEAGUE OF AMERICA 1 (2006)
- CRISIS ON MULTIPLE EARTHS Volume 2
- 52

ALLIANCES:

Justice League of America

THE ORIGIN OF THE SCARECROW

SCOTT BEATTY writer
KELLEY JONES artist
JARED K. FLETCHER letterer
HI-FI colorist
ELISABETH V. GEHRLEIN editor

IN THE WRONG HANDS, *FEAR* CAN BE A WEAPON.

A GANGLY, AWKWARD YOUTH BULLIED FOR HIS RESEMBLANCE TO AUTHOR WASHINGTON IRVING'S ICHABOD CRANE...

...*JONATHAN CRANE* WAS OBSESSED WITH CONQUERING HIS OWN PHOBIAS BY KNOWING THE VERY ESSENCE OF FEAR.

A STUDY OF ANXIETY PARANOIA AND FEAR

WITH A BRIGHT ACADEMIC CAREER IN FRONT OF HIM, CRANE DERAILED HIMSELF FROM THE TENURE-TRACK AT GOTHAM UNIVERSITY...

...BY USING HIS OWN STUDENTS AS UNWILLING PARTICIPANTS IN DANGEROUS FRIGHT-BASED EXPERIMENTS.

CRANE WAS SUMMARILY DISMISSED FROM THE CLASSROOM BY THE BOARD OF REGENTS FOR HIS UNORTHODOX TEACHING METHODS. TO HAVE HIS REVENGE, CRANE PUT HIS KNOWLEDGE OF FEAR TO THE TEST...

PELLED

DISTILLING THE ESSENCE OF TERROR INTO AN AEROSOLIZED FEAR GAS OF HIS OWN DIABOLICAL DESIGN, CRANE CLAD HIMSELF IN STRAW AND SACKCLOTH...

...TO QUITE LITERALLY SCARE THE REGENTS TO DEATH AS *THE SCARECROW!*

IN THEIR COUNTLESS CLASHES, THE SCARECROW HAS ATTEMPTED TO FERRET OUT ANY ANXIETY OR POTENTIAL PHOBIA THAT MIGHT BRING BATMAN TO HIS KNEES.

LITTLE DOES JONATHAN CRANE REALIZE THAT THE DARK KNIGHT'S *WORST FEAR* HAS ALREADY BEEN REALIZED...

AND THE FIRST STEP TO CONQUERING FEAR IS TO FACE IT...

BUT IN GOTHAM CITY, NO FIGURE IS MORE TERRIFYING THAN *THE BATMAN* HIMSELF.

...HEAD-ON...

...LEAVING THE SCARECROW TO PONDER HOW BEST TO ONE DAY DEFEAT THE CAPED CRUSADER AND CRANE'S OWN RECURRING CHIROPTERAPHOBIA...

...FEAR OF BATS!

Powers & Weapons:

THE SCARECROW HAS WEAPONIZED FEAR ITSELF IN THE FORM OF AN ATOMIZED GAS MIXING ADRENO-CORTICO SECRETIONS AND HALLUCINOGENIC COMPOUNDS OF HIS OWN CONCOCTION. WHEN INHALED, THE GAS MAKES A VICTIM'S WORST FEARS FRIGHTENINGLY REAL. ADDITIONALLY, THE SCARECROW PURPORTS TO BE A MASTER OF THE "CRANE STYLE OF VIOLENT DANCING," A MARTIAL ART SUITED TO HIS GANGLY FRAME.

Essential Storylines:

- WORLD'S FINEST COMICS 3
- BATMAN ANNUAL 19
- BATMAN: SCARECROW TALES
- BATMAN: AS THE CROW FLIES

THE ORIGIN OF SINESTRO

WRITER/SCOTT BEATTY
ARTIST/FERNANDO PASARIN
LETTERER/STEVE WANDS
COLORIST/HI-FI
EDITOR/ELISABETH V. GEHRLEIN

POWER *CORRUPTS.*

ON THE WRONG HAND, A POWER RING CAN CORRUPT *ABSOLUTELY.*

SINESTRO OF KORUGAR, ONCE GREEN LANTERN OF SPACE SECTOR 1417, WIELDED HIS RING LIKE NO OTHER PEACEKEEPER IN THE EMPLOY OF THE VENERABLE AND IMMORTAL GUARDIANS OF THE UNIVERSE.

SO SKILLED WAS SINESTRO, HE WAS CHARGED WITH IMPARTING HIS CONSIDERABLE KNOWLEDGE AND EXPERIENCE TO *HAL JORDAN* OF EARTH, NEWLY DRAFTED GREEN LANTERN OF SPACE SECTOR 2814.

BEFORE JORDAN'S INDUCTION INTO THE CORPS, SINESTRO WAS WELL ON HIS WAY TO BECOMING THE GREATEST GREEN LANTERN EVER CHRONICLED IN THE FABLED *BOOK OF OA.*

BUT SINESTRO BELIEVED THAT POLICING THE UNIVERSE REQUIRED A *FORCE OF WILL* GREATER THAN THAT WHICH IMPELLED THE GREEN LANTERNS' MIGHTY POWER RINGS.

AS JORDAN SOON DISCOVERED, SINESTRO KEPT THE PEACE ON PLANET KORUGAR WITH AN EMERALD FIST, A BLATANT AND ARROGANT *ABUSE* OF THE GREAT POWER ENTRUSTED TO HIM.

SUBSEQUENTLY, THE GUARDIANS STRIPPED SINESTRO OF HIS RANK AND PRIVILEGES...

...AND BANISHED HIM TO THE ANTI-MATTER UNIVERSE KNOWN IN INFAMY AS *QWARD.*

DESIRING REVENGE UPON JORDAN AND HIS FORMER MASTERS, A TURNCOAT SINESTRO TRADED GREEN FOR *YELLOW* AS THE COLOR STANDARD OF HIS ALLEGIANCE...

...RETURNING TO THE POSITIVE-MATTER UNIVERSE ARMED WITH A YELLOW POWER RING PROVIDED BY HIS NEW MASTERS: *THE WEAPONERS OF QWARD!*

OF COURSE, AS SINESTRO WELL KNEW, YELLOW WAS THE ONLY COLOR UPON WHICH THE GREEN LANTERNS' RINGS HAD NO EFFECT THANKS TO THE FEAR-MONGERING ENTITY KNOWN AS *PARALLAX!*

THOUGH ONCE HE MIGHT HAVE BEEN THE GREATEST GREEN LANTERN, HE INSTEAD EMBRACED THE ROLE OF THE CORPS' MOST TERRIBLE FOE, SWORN ENEMY OF HAL JORDAN AND A CONSTANT THREAT TO UNIVERSAL STABILITY.

IN BLACKEST DAY, IN BRIGHTEST NIGHT, BEWARE YOUR FEARS MADE INTO LIGHT. LET THOSE WHO TRY TO STOP WHAT'S RIGHT BURN LIKE MY POWER, SINESTRO'S MIGHT!

WITH THE SO-CALLED *SINESTRO CORPS* AFFORDING HIM MORE POWER THAN EVER BEFORE, SINESTRO SPARKED A GALAXY-SPANNING WAR THAT CUT A BLOODY GREEN AND YELLOW SWATH ACROSS SPACE.

ULTIMATELY, THE SINESTRO CORPS WERE DEFEATED, BUT ONLY AFTER FORCING THE GUARDIANS OF THE UNIVERSE TO *REWRITE* THE BOOK OF OA AND ALLOW THEIR STALWART GREEN LANTERNS TO *KILL* IN THE LINE OF DUTY.

HAVING CORRUPTED THE INCORRUPTIBLE, HE THEREFORE BELIEVES THAT WHILE THE GREEN LANTERNS MAY HAVE BEEN VICTORIOUS IN BATTLE, IT WAS *SINESTRO* WHO TRULY *WON THE WAR.*

Powers and Weapons:

SINESTRO IS A BRILLIANT TACTICIAN AND MILITARY STRATEGIST, AS WELL AS A NATURAL WIELDER OF A POWER RING. SINESTRO'S YELLOW POWER RING--LIKE THE GREEN LANTERNS' OWN WILL-POWERED WEAPONS--CAN CREATE ANYTHING SINESTRO CAN IMAGINE. FOR A MIND AS TWISTED AS SINESTRO'S, HIS RING'S CREATIONS CAN BE THE STUFF OF NIGHTMARES.

Affiliations:

- SECRET SOCIETY OF SUPER-VILLAINS
- INJUSTICE LEAGUE
- SINESTRO CORPS

Essential Storylines:

- GREEN LANTERN 7
- GREEN LANTERN: EMERALD DAWN II
- GREEN LANTERN: EMERALD TWILIGHT
- GREEN LANTERN: THE SINESTRO CORPS WAR

THE ORIGIN OF
SOLOMON GRUNDY

WRITER--SCOTT BEATTY
ARTIST--TOM MANDRAKE

LETTERER--TRAVIS LANHAM
COLORIST--HI-FI
EDITOR--ELISABETH V. GEHRLEIN

BORN ON A MONDAY.

CHRISTENED ON TUESDAY.

MARRIED ON WEDNESDAY.

TOOK ILL ON THURSDAY.

WORSE ON FRIDAY.

DIED ON SATURDAY.

BURIED ON SUNDAY.

IS THIS THE END

OF SOLOMON GRUNDY?

POWERS AND WEAPONS:
WHEN CYRUS GOLD WAS MURDERED AND SUBMERGED IN SLAUGHTER SWAMP, THE PARLIAMENT OF TREES ATTEMPTED TO RESURRECT HIM AS EARTH'S LATEST PLANT ELEMENTAL. BUT SINCE GOLD DID NOT DIE BY FIRE--A KEY ELEMENT IN THE CREATION OF SUCH A PRIMAL SPIRIT--HE WAS INSTEAD REBORN AS A NEAR-MINDLESS ZOMBIE WITH MURDEROUS INTENT, DUBBED SOLOMON GRUNDY BY HOBOS WHO FIRST ENCOUNTERED HIM. SUPERSTRONG AND POTENTIALLY IMMORTAL GIVEN HIS REPEATED CYCLE OF DEATH AND RESURRECTION, GRUNDY'S MOST RECENT INCARNATION IS HIGHLY INTELLIGENT, MAKING HIM ALL THE MORE DANGEROUS.

ESSENTIAL STORYLINES:
JUSTICE LEAGUE OF AMERICA: THE TORNADO'S PATH
GREEN ARROW 18, 53
SECRET SIX

AFFILIATIONS:
SECRET SOCIETY OF SUPER-VILLAINS
INJUSTICE SOCIETY OF THE WORLD
INJUSTICE LEAGUE

THE Origin OF

Starfire

Writer – MARK WAID
Artist – JOE BENITEZ
Colorist – ALEX SINCLAIR
Letterer – ROB LEIGH
Asst. Editor – HARVEY RICHARDS
Assoc. Editor – JEANINE SCHAEFER
Editor – MICHAEL SIGLAIN

Starfire Created by
MARV WOLFMAN and GEORGE PÉREZ

PRINCESS KORIAND'R GREW UP ON THE IDYLLIC, HEDONISTIC WORLD OF TAMARAN. THERE, KORY WAS BELOVED AND GAVE LOVE IN RETURN--

--A VIRTUE NOT SHARED BY HER BITTER OLDER SISTER, PRINCESS KOMAND'R, WHO GREW DARK WITH PSYCHOPATHIC JEALOUSY THAT KORY, NOT SHE, WAS THE HEIR APPARENT TO THE THRONE.

BETRAYING HER PEOPLE, KOMAND'R ALLIED WITH THE MILITARISTIC CITADEL, HELPING THEM TO CONQUER THE TAMARANEANS AND ALLOWING THEM TO LIVE UNDER ONE CONDITION:

THAT KORIAND'R BE DELIVERED INTO SLAVERY.

KOMAND'R SALIVATED AT THE PROSPECT OF SISTERLY VENGEANCE.

KORIAND'R, TRAINED IN WARRIOR WAYS AS A CHILD, ENDURED YEARS OF TORTURE TO SAVE HER FAMILY--

--PAIN MAGNIFIED ONCE SHE AND KOMAND'R WERE IN TURN CAPTURED BY THE SADISTIC PSIONS, WHO TURNED THE SISTERS INTO LAB ANIMALS--

--AND, UNWITTINGLY, HANDED KORIAND'R THE KEYS TO HER CHAINS.

USING THE STARBOLT POWERS GRANTED HER BY A PSION EXPERIMENT, STARFIRE ESCAPED CAPTIVITY.

LIGHT-YEARS FROM HOME, SHE FLED TO THE NEAREST PLANET--

--WHERE SHE JOINED WITH ITS TEEN TITANS TO SAVE EARTH FROM A CITADEL INVASION.

RECHRISTENED "STARFIRE" BY HER TEAMMATES, SHE MADE THIS NEW WORLD HER HOME.

UTTERLY BOMBASTIC AND UTTERLY UNAPOLOGETIC, STARFIRE IS GENTLE WITH HER FRIENDS AND BARBARIC WITH HER FOES. HER CLOSEST BOND HAS ALWAYS BEEN WITH DICK GRAYSON--

--THE ONLY TITAN ACCUSTOMED TO HAVING A PARTNER THAT INTIMIDATING.

POWERS AND WEAPONS:

Starfire channels solar energy into starbolt blasts, super-strength, moderate invulnerability, flight, and the ability to travel through the vacuum of space under her own power and without need of a spacesuit.
She is also a deadly hand-to-hand combatant and can absorb languages through touch.

ESSENTIAL STORYLINES:

- New Teen Titans Archives
- New Teen Titans: The Judas Contract
- Cosmic Odyssey
- 52

ALLIANCES:

- Teen Titans

MIKAAL TOMAS STARMAN

LEN WEIN - writer   SERGIO CARRERA - artist
PETE PANTAZIS - colors   SAL CIPRIANO - letters
ADAM SCHLAGMAN - editor

...EVEN AT THE VERY BEGINNING, AMONG HIS WARLIKE ALIEN RACE, MIKAAL TOMAS WAS ONE OF A KIND...

WHEN THE WOMAN HE LOVED WAS *MURDERED* WHILE ATTEMPTING TO *WARN* THE EARTH OF HIS RACE'S IMPENDING INVASION, MIKAAL TOOK UP HER *CAUSE*...

QUICKLY *CAPTURED* AND SENTENCED TO DEATH, MIKAAL *ESCAPED* HIS CAPTORS AND FLED TO *EARTH*--

--WHERE HE SOON LEARNED THAT HUMANS WERE NOT QUITE SO *PEACE-LOVING* AS HE'D BEEN LED TO BELIEVE.

MIKAAL, SEDUCED BY THE WAYS OF EARTH, SPENT THE NEXT SEVERAL YEARS GOING FROM *VICE* TO *VICE*, AS HE STRUGGLED TO REDISCOVER HIS OWN *IDENTITY*--

--UNTIL THE NIGHT HE WAS CONFRONTED BY HIS OLDEST FOE, WHO TOLD MIKAAL THAT THEY TWO WERE NOW THE LAST OF THEIR RACE--

--AND THEN FOUGHT MIKAAL TO THE DEATH, LEAVING MIKAAL'S SONIC CRYSTAL EMBEDDED IN HIS CHEST--

--AND MIKAAL NOW AND FOREVER TRULY ALONE.

IT WAS THEREFORE NO SURPRISE THAT NO ONE NOTICED HIM GONE WHEN HE WAS DRUGGED AND KIDNAPPED--

--AND SPENT THE NEXT SEVERAL YEARS BEING PASSED FROM HAND TO HAND AS LITTLE MORE THAN A GROTESQUE CURIOSITY--

--WHICH IS PRECISELY WHAT HE WAS WHEN JACK KNIGHT, THE LATEST INCARNATION OF STARMAN, FOUND HIM ON DISPLAY AT A RUN-DOWN CARNIVAL...

TODAY, TO SLAKE HIS RACE'S BATTLE-HUNGER THAT HAS BEEN REAWAKENED WITHIN HIM, MIKAAL FIGHTS CRIME AS A WOULD-BE SUPER-HERO--

--ON A NEVER-ENDING QUEST TO FIND JUSTICE AT LAST!

POWERS AND WEAPONS:

THE LAST SURVIVOR OF THE PLANET TALOK III, MIKAAL TOMAS POSSESSES SUPER-HUMAN STRENGTH AND THE POWER OF FLIGHT. MIKAAL ALSO HAS A UNIQUE SONIC CRYSTAL EMBEDDED IN HIS CHEST, WHICH ALLOWS HIM TO FIRE CONCENTRATED BEAMS OF ENERGY.

ALLIANCES:

• JUSTICE LEAGUE OF AMERICA

ESSENTIAL STORYLINES:

• FIRST ISSUE SPECIAL # 12
• JUSTICE LEAGUE: CRY FOR JUSTICE
• STARMAN OMNIBUS VOLUMES 1, 2, 5, 6

THE ORIGIN OF STEEL

MARK WAID·WRITER · JON BOGDANOVE·ART

ALEX SINCLAIR·COLORS · NICK J. NAPOLITANO·LETTERS

HARVEY RICHARDS · ASST. EDITOR · STEPHEN WACKER EDITOR

STEEL CREATED BY LOUISE SIMONSON & JON BOGDANOVE

I OWE YOU MY LIFE...!

THEN MAKE IT COUNT.

THOSE WERE THE WORDS THAT FORGED JOHN HENRY IRONS INTO A HERO.

RECRUITED OUT OF COLLEGE BY THE INDUSTRIAL FIRM **AMERTEK**, IRONS ALLOWED HIS LOVE OF ENGINEERING TO OVERRIDE HIS SENSE OF ETHICS AS HE DESIGNED ADVANCED WEAPONS SYSTEMS--

--THAT HIS CORRUPT BOSSES SOLD TO TERRORISTS.

HORRIFIED BY WHAT HE HAD WROUGHT, IRONS WENT INTO HIDING, LABORING IN CONSTRUCTION AND LIVING IN FEAR UNDER AN ASSUMED NAME.

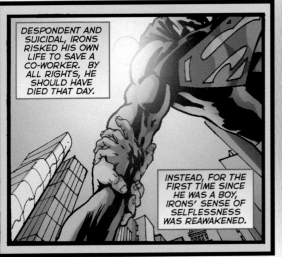

DESPONDENT AND SUICIDAL, IRONS RISKED HIS OWN LIFE TO SAVE A CO-WORKER. BY ALL RIGHTS, HE SHOULD HAVE DIED THAT DAY.

INSTEAD, FOR THE FIRST TIME SINCE HE WAS A BOY, IRONS' SENSE OF SELFLESSNESS WAS REAWAKENED.

ADOPTING SUPERMAN'S SYMBOL, IRONS NOT ONLY FOUND THE COURAGE TO RECLAIM HIS IDENTITY AND FACE HIS PAST--

--HE JOINED SUPERMAN'S NEVER-ENDING BATTLE FOR TRUTH AND JUSTICE AS **STEEL**, THE ARMORED AVENGER.

YEARS OF HEROISM CAME AT A PRICE, HOWEVER, WHEN LEX LUTHOR EXPOSED IRONS TO GENETIC TAMPERING, TRANSFORMING STEEL'S SKIN INTO LIQUID METAL.

LUTHOR BELIEVED IT WOULD BE THE END OF STEEL. INSTEAD, AS ALWAYS, IRONS SUMMONED THE WILL TO RISE ABOVE ADVERSITY AND USES HIS POWER TO FIGHT HARDER THAN EVER FOR THE GOOD OF THE COMMON MAN.

POWERS AND WEAPONS:

John Henry Irons can, at will, turn his skin into stainless steel, which increases his strength and makes him virtually indestructable.

In combat, Steel wields a hammer whose kinetic energy increases with distance thrown. Hurled 20 yards, it can stop a car; hurled 60, it can crush a tank.

ESSENTIAL STORYLINES:

· THE RETURN OF SUPERMAN
· STEEL: THE FORGING OF A HERO
· 52

THE ORIGIN OF SUPERMAN

LEN WEIN
writer

GARY FRANK
artist

BRAD ANDERSON
colors

SAL CIPRIANO
letters

ADAM SCHLAGMAN
editor

SUPERMAN *created by*
JERRY SIEGEL *and*
JOE SHUSTER

BY NOW, EVERYONE HAS HEARD THE STORY...

REALIZING HIS BELOVED HOMEWORLD WAS *DOOMED*, A SCIENTIST NAMED JOR-EL SENT HIS INFANT SON KAL-EL ROCKETING IN THE DIRECTION OF OUR *EARTH* MERE INSTANTS BEFORE KRYPTON *EXPLODED*...

THE INFANT'S EXPERIMENTAL STARSHIP ULTIMATELY CRASH-LANDED IN A KANSAS CORNFIELD, WHERE IT WAS DISCOVERED BY A KINDLY FARM COUPLE, *JONATHAN* AND *MARTHA* KENT...

WANTING A FAMILY, THE KENTS TOOK THE INFANT IN AND RAISED HIM AS THEIR OWN, NAMING HIM *CLARK*, AND IMBUING HIM WITH THE STAUNCH CODE OF ETHICS AND MORALITY THAT DEFINES HIM TO THIS DAY...

AS HE GREW, THE BOY DISCOVERED HE POSSESSED POWERS AND ABILITIES FAR *BEYOND* THOSE OF NORMAL MEN...

HE CAN CHANGE THE COURSE OF MIGHTY *RIVERS*...

...BEND *STEEL* IN HIS BARE HANDS....

TODAY, DISGUISED AS A MILD-MANNERED *REPORTER* FOR THE DAILY PLANET, A GREAT METROPOLITAN NEWSPAPER...

HE FIGHTS A NEVER-ENDING BATTLE FOR *TRUTH* AND *JUSTICE*...

...THE *ONLY* WAY HE KNOWS *HOW!*

POWERS AND WEAPONS:

POSSESSED OF A WIDE ARRAY OF EXTRAORDINARY POWERS--FLIGHT, SUPER-STRENGTH, INVULNERABILITY, TELESCOPIC, MICROSCOPIC AND HEAT-VISION, SUPER-HEARING, MANY OTHERS-- THE MAN OF STEEL'S GREATEST WEAPON REMAINS HIS HONEST, UNWAVERING HEART.

ALLIANCES:

JUSTICE LEAGUE OF AMERICA
THE LEGION OF SUPER-HEROES

ESSENTIAL STORYLINES:

- SUPERMAN: SECRET ORIGIN
- SUPERMAN: BRAINIAC
- DEATH AND RETURN OF SUPERMAN
- SUPERMAN: NEW KRYPTON
- SUPERMAN: LAST SON
- WHATEVER HAPPENED TO THE MAN OF TOMORROW
- SUPERMAN/BATMAN: PUBLIC ENEMIES

THE ORIGIN OF THE TEEN TITANS

WRITER—MARK WAID
ARTIST—KARL KERSCHL
COLORIST—STEPHANE PERU
LETTERER—KEN LOPEZ
ASST. EDITOR—HARVEY RICHARDS
ASSOC. EDITOR—JEANINE SCHAEFER
EDITOR—MICHAEL SIGLAIN

VICTOR STONE ALWAYS PAYS HIS DEBTS.

NEARLY KILLED AS A YOUNG MAN BY A LAB ACCIDENT, VIC WAS REBUILT AS A HALF-HUMAN CYBORG AND DRAFTED BY THE TEEN TITANS--

--A "JUNIOR JUSTICE LEAGUE" WHO HELPED VIC CHANNEL HIS RAGE AND DESPAIR INTO HEROISM.

THAT ACT OF KINDNESS SAVED VIC'S LIFE AND MADE THE WORLD A BETTER PLACE. WITHOUT THE TITANS' INTERVENTION, HIS WOULD HAVE BEEN A MUCH DARKER PATH.

OVER TIME, THE TEAM MATURED, AS DID VIC, WHO HELPED HOLD IT TOGETHER THROUGH SEVERAL INCARNATIONS UNTIL ITS CATACLYSMIC END--

--WHEN A ROGUE SUPERMAN ROBOT CUT A MURDEROUS SWATH THROUGH BOTH THE TITANS AND THE GROUP THEY'D INSPIRED, YOUNG JUSTICE.

THOSE WHO SURVIVED STAYED SOLO. BUT IN ORDER TO FIND A LIFELINE TO THE FUTURE...

...HE WOULD HAVE TO REMEMBER THE PAST.

THERE, HE PROVIDED THE NEW GENERATION OF YOUNG HEROES A PLACE TO BELONG, JUST AS OTHERS HAD ONCE DONE FOR HIM. SO LONG AS HE HAS ANYTHING TO SAY ABOUT IT, THERE WILL ALWAYS BE A TEEN TITANS.

VICTOR STONE ALWAYS PAYS HIS DEBTS.

WITH THE COOPERATION OF CITY OFFICIALS, VIC DESIGNED AND BUILT A NEW TITANS TOWER OFF THE COAST OF SAN FRANCISCO.

CURRENT MEMBERSHIP:

SSENTIAL STORYLINES:

ITANS/YOUNG JUSTICE: Graduation Day
EEN TITANS: A Kids' Game
EEN TITANS: Family Lost
EEN TITANS: Life and Death

MISS MARTIAN

JERICHO

RAVEN

RAVAGER

KID DEVIL

ROBIN

WONDER GIRL

CYBORG

THE ORIGIN OF THE TRICKSTER

Prisoner #F113-90125: James Jesse

Writer **SCOTT BEATTY**
Artist **ETHAN VAN SCIVER**

SON OF CIRCUS AERIALISTS THE FLYING JESSES, YOUNG JAMES CONQUERED A FEAR OF HEIGHTS...

...BY DEVELOPING GRAVITY-DEFYING "AIR-WALKER" SHOES GUARANTEED NEVER TO LET HIM FALL FROM THE HIGH-WIRE.

RATHER THAN USE HIS INVENTION FOR LEGITIMATE FAME, JAMES JESSE PREFERRED TO WALK IN THE FOOTSTEPS OF HIS NEFARIOUS "NAMESAKE" AND BECAME A MASKED MALCONTENT...

...KNOWN INFAMOUSLY AS THE TRICKSTER.

AS A FOUNDING MEMBER OF THE FLASH'S "ROGUES GALLERY" OF FREQUENT FOES, TRICKSTER HAS BATTLED *THREE* SCARLET SPEEDSTERS DURING HIS LONG CRIMINAL CAREER...

AND SUCCEEDED IN KILLING THE LATEST.

SUMMARILY ARRESTED BY THE SO-CALLED "SUICIDE SQUAD"--FELLOW VILLAINS AWARDED AMNESTY IN EXCHANGE FOR GOVERNMENT SERVICE--TRICKSTER AND PIPER RECENTLY ESCAPED FEDERAL CUSTODY.

Powers & Weapons:

TRICKSTER'S BAG OF DEADLY TRICKS INCLUDES HIS "AIR-WALKER" SHOES AND A VARIETY OF BOOBY-TRAPPED TOYS, INCLUDING EXPLOSIVE RUBBER CHICKENS OR RAZOR-SHARP YO-YOS.

Essential Storylines:

- THE FLASH: ROGUE WAR
- THE FLASH: FASTEST MAN ALIVE #13
- COUNTDOWN

THE ORIGIN OF the Pied Piper

Colorist HI-FI
Letterer JARED K. FLETCHER
Editor ELISABETH V. GEHRLEIN

Prisoner #F106-OU812:
Hartley Rathaway

SON OF PUBLISHING MAGNATE OSGOOD RATHAWAY, YOUNG HARTLEY SUFFERED CONGENITAL DEAFNESS...

...THAT WAS EVENTUALLY CURED THANKS TO HIS PARENTS' DEEP POCKETS AND COUNTLESS SURGERIES.

BORED BY ALL OTHER PURSUITS, WEALTHY HARTLEY RATHAWAY USED HIS NEWLY ACQUIRED EAR FOR MUSIC IN ALL ITS FORMS TO PLAY SINISTER SOUR NOTES...

...AS A MODERN-DAY MESMERIZING PIED PIPER.

PRIOR TO HIS ALLEGED COMPLICITY IN THE MURDER OF THE FLASH, PIPER HAD MADE CONCERTED EFFORTS TO REFORM, EVEN BEFRIENDING ONE OF THE FASTEST MEN ALIVE.

BOTH ROGUES ARE CONSIDERED ARMED AND DANGEROUS, AND MAY LIKELY BE TRAVELING TOGETHER.

Powers & Weapons:

A GENIUS IN THE SCIENCE OF SONICS, PIPER HAS INVENTED A VARIETY OF SOUND WEAPONS ABLE TO HYPNOTIZE ANYONE WITHIN EARSHOT OR GENERATE HIGH-PITCHED DESTRUCTIVE FORCE FROM A SINGLE MUSICAL NOTE.

Essential Storylines:

- THE FLASH: IRON HEIGHTS
- COUNTDOWN SPECIAL: THE FLASH 80-PAGE GIANT
- COUNTDOWN

THE ORIGIN OF TWO-FACE

BAIL BONDS

MARK WAID-WRITER
MARK CHIARELLO-ARTIST
NICK J. NAPOLITANO-LETTERER
ELISABETH V. GEHRLEIN-EDITOR

AN ABUSED AND SCHIZOPHRENIC CHILD, HARVEY DENT LEARNED TO HIDE HIS DARK RAGE BENEATH A DEVOTION TO LAW AND ORDER.

AS GOTHAM CITY'S FIREBRAND DISTRICT ATTORNEY AND WITH BATMAN AS HIS ALLY, HARVEY WAS ABLE TO KEEP HIS SECRET MADNESS IN CHECK...

...UNTIL THE DAY A VENGEFUL MOB BOSS HURLED ACID IN HIS FACE...

D.A. DENT: PRIDE OF GOTHAM CITY

...SCARRING IT HORRIFICALLY.

THE TRAUMA OF THE ASSAULT PERMANENTLY UNBALANCED DENT, TRANSFORMING HIM INTO TWO-FACE, A FRACTURED VILLAIN OBSESSED WITH DUALITY.

HIS EVERY DECISION IS DICTATED BY THE TOSS OF A TWO-HEADED COIN SCRATCHED ON ONE SIDE. HALF THE TIME, THE COIN'S FLIP FORCES DENT TO ACT HONORABLY...

...BUT WHEN THE COIN'S SCARRED FACE TURNS UP...

...EVIL WINS OUT.

DENT'S TRADEMARK CRIMES ALWAYS REVOLVE AROUND THE NUMBER TWO...

GOTHAM EVENING HERALD

DOUBLE MURDERS!

WEALTHY TWINS KIDNAPPED
THE GOTHAM CITY DAILY JOURNAL

DOUBLE DIAMOND ROBBED

...BUT MOST OF THE TIME, IT TAKES ONLY ONE MAN TO STOP HIM.

Powers & Weapons:

TWO-FACE IS A GIFTED MASTERMIND OBSESSED WITH THE NUMBER TWO, HIS CRIMINAL MOTIF. HIS EVERY DECISION IS DETERMINED BY THE FLIP OF HIS TWO-SIDED COIN.

Essential Storylines:

- BATMAN ANNUAL 14
- BATMAN: FACES
- BATMAN: THE LONG HALLOWEEN
- BATMAN: FACE THE FACE

THE ORIGIN OF WILDCAT

MARK WAID · *Writer*
JERRY ORDWAY · *Art*
ALEX SINCLAIR · *Color*
ROB LEIGH · *Letters*
STEPHEN WACKER &
HARVEY RICHARDS · *Editors*

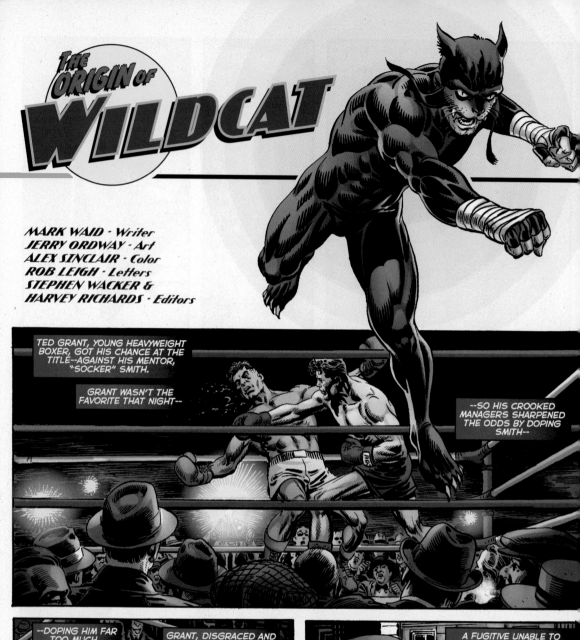

TED GRANT, YOUNG HEAVYWEIGHT BOXER, GOT HIS CHANCE AT THE TITLE--AGAINST HIS MENTOR, "SOCKER" SMITH.

GRANT WASN'T THE FAVORITE THAT NIGHT--

--SO HIS CROOKED MANAGERS SHARPENED THE ODDS BY DOPING SMITH--

--DOPING HIM FAR TOO MUCH.

GRANT, DISGRACED AND FRAMED FOR MURDER, FLED FROM THE LAW.

A FUGITIVE UNABLE TO SHOW HIS FACE IN PUBLIC, GRANT--INSPIRED BY AMERICA'S NEW "MYSTERY MEN"--WAS DRIVEN IN DESPERATION TO CREATE A NEW IDENTITY FOR HIMSELF.

AS WILDCAT, HE APPREHENDED SMITH'S TRUE KILLERS, PROVING HIS INNOCENCE--

--AND REALIZING THE ADRENALINE RUSH THAT COMES WITH DELIVERING BARE-KNUCKLED JUSTICE.

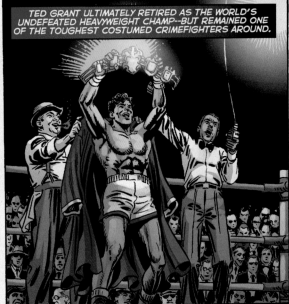

TED GRANT ULTIMATELY RETIRED AS THE WORLD'S UNDEFEATED HEAVYWEIGHT CHAMP--BUT REMAINED ONE OF THE TOUGHEST COSTUMED CRIMEFIGHTERS AROUND.

IN HIS DAY, WILDCAT TRAINED BATMAN, BLACK CANARY, CATWOMAN AND EVEN SUPERMAN IN THE "SWEET SCIENCE" OF BOXING--

--AND TODAY HE TEACHES A NEW GENERATION OF SUPER-HEROES AS THE CO-CHAIRMAN OF THE JUSTICE SOCIETY OF AMERICA.

POWERS AND WEAPONS:

Wildcat, the finest boxer who ever lived, has studied and mastered a wide range of less traditional fighting styles as well, including Muai Thai, Capoeira, Krav Maga and Hapkaido.

He is also a skilled motorcyclist.

ESSENTIAL STORYLINES:

- SENSATION COMICS 1
- JSA CLASSIFIED 8-9
- BATMAN/ WILDCAT 1-3

ALLIANCES:

Justice Society of America

THE ORIGIN OF WONDER WOMAN

MARK WAID-WRITER
ADAM HUGHES-ART
LAURA MARTIN-COLORS
NICK J. NAPOLITANO-LETTERS
HARVEY RICHARDS-ASST. EDITOR
STEPHEN WACKER-EDITOR
SPECIAL THANKS TO MARK CHIARELLO
WONDER WOMAN CREATED BY
WILLIAM MOULTON MARSTON

FOR CENTURIES, THE RACE OF WARRIOR WOMEN KNOWN AS THE AMAZONS SECLUDED THEMSELVES ON THE REMOTE ISLAND OF THEMYSCIRA.

OVER THE YEARS, UNDER THE TUTELAGE OF THE GODDESS APHRODITE AND THEIR QUEEN, HIPPOLYTA, THE AMAZONS MASTERED THE PEACEFUL TEACHINGS OF GAEA, THE EARTH MOTHER.

EVENTUALLY, HIPPOLYTA'S PRAYERS FOR A DAUGHTER WHO COULD FULLY EMBODY THE AMAZON SPIRIT WERE GRANTED.

THE GRECIAN GODS COMMANDED HIPPOLYTA TO CARVE THE CHILD OF HER DREAMS FROM CLAY--

--THEN BROUGHT THE INFANT TO LIFE, GIFTING THE PRINCESS DIANA WITH POWERS AND ABILITIES EQUAL TO THEIR OWN.

AS SHE GREW, DIANA CONTINUALLY IMPRESSED EVEN THE AMAZONS WITH HER STRENGTH, SPEED AND HUNTING PROWESS--

--MAKING HER, WHEN SHE CAME OF AGE, THE NATURAL CHOICE TO DELIVER THE MESSAGE OF GAEA AND THEMYSCIRA TO THE OUTSIDE WORLD.

DONNING A UNIFORM DECORATED WITH SYMBOLS REPRESENTING A LEGENDARY AMAZON HEROINE, DIANA BROUGHT HER COURAGE AND SKILLS FULLY TO BEAR AS WONDER WOMAN, AMBASSADOR OF PEACE.

NOW, GUIDED BY AN INDOMITABLE WILL AND A COMPASSIONATE HEART, SHE FIGHTS TO PROTECT INNOCENTS EVERYWHERE FROM THE FORCES OF TYRANNY.

POWERS AND WEAPONS:

Wonder Woman possesses godlike strength, speed, invulnerability, and the ability to fly. She is a skilled swordswoman and, like her namesake, is a master of the hunt and at communing with animals.

Wonder Woman's arsenal includes a magic lasso which compels its captives to speak the truth, a boomerang tiara that can cut through diamond, and bracelets that can deflect gunfire.

ESSENTIAL STORYLINES:
- WONDER WOMAN Archives Vol. 1-4
- WONDER WOMAN: Gods and Mortals
- WONDER WOMAN: The Hiketeia
- WONDER WOMAN: Eyes of the Gorgon

ALLIANCES:
Justice League of America

THE ORIGIN OF ZATANNA

WRITER-MARK WAID
ART AND COLOR-BRIAN BOLLAND
LETTERER-TRAVIS LANHAM
ASST. EDITOR-HARVEY RICHARDS
ASSOC. EDITOR-JEANINE SCHAEFER
EDITOR-MICHAEL SIGLAIN

ZATANNA CREATED
BY GARDNER FOX

LIKE ANY GOOD STAGE MAGICIAN, JOHN ZATARA NEVER REVEALED HIS SECRETS.

HIS DAUGHTER, ZATANNA, KNEW THAT HER FATHER HAD ONCE FOUGHT CRIME AS A FULL-FLEDGED SORCERER, BUT THE TRUTH BEHIND HIS ABILITIES REMAINED A MYSTERY TO HER...

...UNTIL THE DAY HE VANISHED, KIDNAPPED BY AN OLD FOE. INVESTIGATING HIS DISAPPEARANCE, ZATANNA DELVED INTO HER FATHER'S LIBRARY...

...AND LEARNED FOR THE FIRST TIME OF HER ANCESTORS, A LONG LINE OF HISTORICAL WIZARDS FROM ARION THE ATLANTEAN TO SINDELLA OF THE ANCIENT *HOMO MAGI* RACE.

MOREOVER, ZATANNA TAUGHT HERSELF HOW TO TAP INTO HER GENETICALLY INHERITED POWERS:

ELDNAC
NRUB.

BY SPEAKING HER SPELLS *BACKWARDS.*

ZATANNA'S LONG QUEST FOR ZATARA WAS SUCCESSFUL...BUT ONLY WITH THE ASSISTANCE OF SEVERAL NOTEWORTHY SUPER-HEROES.

INSPIRED BY THEIR SELFLESSNESS, ZATANNA ASPIRED TO JOIN THEIR RANKS AND WAS EVENTUALLY INDUCTED INTO THE JUSTICE LEAGUE OF AMERICA.

DURING HER TENURE, ZATANNA WAS SOMETIMES CALLED UPON TO ERASE DANGEROUS INFORMATION FROM THE MINDS OF THE LEAGUE'S ENEMIES.

THE QUESTIONABLE ETHICS OF HER "MIND WIPES" ALARMED SOME LEAGUERS, CREATING TRUST ISSUES WHICH EVENTUALLY HELPED DRIVE HER FROM THE TEAM.

SINCE THEN, ZATANNA HAS REBUILT HER REPUTATION AS ONE OF EARTH'S FOREMOST SENTINELS AGAINST MYSTIC THREATS. IT WASN'T HARD.

SNIAHC DNIB EEHT!

SHE'S MAGIC THAT WAY.

POWERS AND WEAPONS:

ZATANNA CAN CAST POWERFUL SPELLS AND INCANTATIONS BY DESCRIBING THEIR EFFECTS IN REVERSE-WORD SPEECH--FOR EXAMPLE, "STELLUB TLEM" OR "NAMREPUS RAEPPA!"

ESSENTIAL STORYLINES:

·JLA: ZATANNA'S SEARCH
·SEVEN SOLDIERS: ZATANNA
·IDENTITY CRISIS

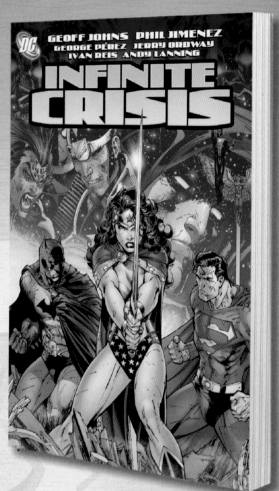

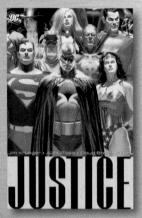